Under the Wheel of History

of History

A Woman's Journey through the Twentieth Century

Alexander Kugushev

Table of Contents

Finding mother's ailing father. Stresses and perils under German occupation. American bombings.

The Soviets approach.   Mother flees again, with her son. Adventurous journey and Gestapo border. Survival in Vienna in 1944–45, under bombs and the protection of Sweden. Soviets again and flight once more.

Threading her way through disintegrating Germany in March/ April 1945.   Adventurous final days: my mother conveys me into Switzerland and stays in Austria, working for the French occupation forces.   Rescuing her father from communist Yugoslavia. Decision to leave Europe forever.

Choosing Argentina.   Arrival in Buenos Aires, death of her father. Difficult adaptation; starting a language school, romance. Moving on to the United States, starting another language school in her sixties; travels and final years.

List of illustrations:

Acknowledgements:

This book's final form owes much to the sagacious advice and to the editorial recommendations of Phyllis Gray and Bea and Bob Gormley. For this and for their encouragement I thank them. They have improved me as an author.

My Mother and Her Turbulent Times

My mother, Anna Lapinskaia, was born to Russian parents in Paris, in April 1900. She died in California, in September 1989, four short weeks before the Berlin Wall collapsed. Her birth coincided with that of the twentieth century; her death with that of its historical, if not its calendric, ending. She thus arched over the demise, in cataclysmic steps, of the residues of a medieval world and the emergence of an as yet uncertain new one. Her memoir provides this book's structural backbone; her century's tempestuous history the context of her life.

> *It is the ideas and sentiments which pervade a people that are the true cause of everything else. Alexis de Tocqueville*

At my mother's birth, an era was speeding towards its ending. Traditional political structures — monarchies and empires — still dominated the world. The twentieth century would sweep away most kings, emperors and aristocrats, along with their morning coats and their servants galore, often traumatically for my mother. She would spend much of her life beset by eruptions of unprecedented, mostly virulent ideologies.

1

The initial part of my mother's memoir reflects an advantaged upbringing as part of Russia's well-to-do gentry and a correspondingly limited worldview. The conditions in which she grew up were perhaps not much different than those of affluent Americans of that period; Teddy Roosevelt's childhood comes to mind. But beginning in 1917 and for the subsequent three decades, her life rolled on as a constant adventure film. As the wheels of twentieth century turned, amoral and often demonic men reached for power. After 1918, ferocious nationalisms clashed with totalitarian forms of socialism and with liberal capitalism. In this swirl, the Russia which bore my mother disappeared.

The Russian Revolution of 1917 upended her life. As her memoir progresses, she begins to reflect an awakening to new realities that neither she nor anyone else in 1900 could imagine. She was born into an ideological bundle, not dissimilar from that of most people living before 1914. In her case, it consisted of received beliefs in Russia's imperial destiny and of Russian Orthodox faith, both deeply nationalistic. She grew up surrounded by monarchist and conservative ideas prevalent in her social class. But as she matured and considered the reasons for Russia's revolution, she evolved a more democratic outlook and brought me up in that spirit. She believed that a constitutional monarchy could have saved Russia from the eventual horrors of communism.

She wrote her memoir from the perspective she knew. By 1989, the year of her death, the events of the twentieth century had fully disassembled the universe into which she was born. Over a century after her birth, we live in a different universe which makes much of her initial thinking hard to comprehend. As she witnessed the twentieth century's demolition derby, she kept adjusting her thinking, not always understanding the nature of the change, or sympathizing with it.

෬

I remember her in her prime as of medium height, brown-haired, brown-eyed, not bad looking to her son, with a roundish, southern-Russian face. She grew up in the shadow of an overwhelmingly accomplished father and of the doting attention lavished on her brilliant younger brother, whom she adored. For those reasons, but also perhaps because less was expected from girls, my mother lived burdened by a fairly low self-esteem.

She was a woman of formidable self-discipline and spirit of sacrifice, and her sense of duty in bringing me up drove her through thick and thin. She was cultured and endeavored early on to expose me, with checkered success, to Botticelli, Dürer, Michelangelo, to Russian literature classics, to Mozart, Beethoven, and Mussorgsky. And she wanted me to know languages. She also had a sense of humor and, despite often dire circumstances, I grew up on a constant diet of jokes, puns and witticisms. Her life was tragic, though she was too stoic to admit it. Her memoir was written in Russian. Its title page says:

Under the Wheel of History
Memories
To my son and friend
Anna Kugusheva
Menlo Park, California, 1988

My mother's memoir, all too often laconic, consists of diary portions she had maintained throughout her life. Her tone is objective, almost detached, and she grows reticent about some of the least happy times of her life. Toward her end she endeavored to bring it all in order and completed this memoir four days before dying. In the text that follows, *her words appear in italics, in indented paragraphs.* My contextual cultural and historical commentary appears in roman type, running the full width of the page.

Family photos took first priority among what my mother packed in all her escapes and migrations. She carried her past with her and I have inherited hundreds of photos, some going back to the nineteenth century. They complement much of what she doesn't say in her memoir. From this morgue of family memories, rescued from wars, revolutions, retreats, and escapes, I include, in the middle section of this book, some glimpses of her life.

Favored Childhood Amid Gathering Storms

My mother speaks:

*H**ow to begin a memoir? Russian émigré newspapers recommend not to dwell on personal matters, but to speak of issues — large and small — that define our age. While still a child, I remember asking my mother, "What is history?" Her answer distressed me, "The times of great events have passed and I, her daughter, would have to content myself with a quiet, uninteresting life." Since then I have concluded that a memoir concerns personal matters, of course, but also that they acquire sharper meaning when painted on the broader canvas of history. Historical events, large and small, have defined my life to an extent my mother, or perhaps anyone else, could not have imagined at the beginning of the twentieth century.*

My father, Mikhail Nikitich Lapinski, was a professor at Kiev University and held the chair in neuropathology and psychiatry. We lived with my mother, Maria Aleksandrovna Lapinskaia, my

*paternal grandmother, and my brother Nikita in Kiev, on Bulevarno
Kudriavskaia 27.*

A century later, in 2004, I visited that house. To my great surprise, it
remains as my mother remembered it and as it appears in her surviving
prerevolutionary photos. The communists had made it the administration
building for the huge hospital they built in the garden behind it. It
continues now in that function, in a new country called Ukraine. I stood
in her large, light and airy bedroom, with tall windows and still painted
in pastels, and in my grandfather's oak-paneled study, absorbing their
lives as I knew them through what they had so lovingly described.

My grandfather was always attracted to the cutting edge of progress.
A profoundly cultured man, conversant in several languages, with a
near doctorate degree in history, in addition to a medical degree, he
specialized in the then nascent field of neuropsychiatry.

My mother Assia (Anna) was born in France, where my grandfather
pursued postdoctoral research. A few months later they returned to
their home in Kiev. Their large house had a staff of servants, a butler,
and a coachman, the latter in time replaced by a chauffeur. Behind
the house extended a considerable shaded garden, with old trees and
a somewhat wild ravine with a little bridge over it. That is where now
stands the Soviet-built hospital.

My grandfather issued from landed gentry of Polish descent. What is
now the Ukraine belonged to Poland in the seventeenth century, when
his ancestors settled there. When these territories united with Russia
later in that century, the Lapinskis stayed, became Greek Orthodox, and
Russianized completely.

Assia's mother issued from a family of Muscovite merchants and
industrialists, the Kornilovs. Prerevolutionary Russia's population
consisted of an ocean of poor, brutalized, ignorant peasantry, a few
wealthy peasants, a small aristocracy and landholding gentry, the last
two often idle and unproductive, and of an even smaller bourgeoisie
of entrepreneurial merchants and industrialists. The latter largely
resided in Moscow, the ancient capital, distant culturally and politically
from St. Petersburg. The Kornilovs belonged to these capitalistic clans,
which arose in the sixteenth and seventeenth centuries. Some were
fabulously rich, like the Morosovs, the Tretiakovs, and the Stroganovs

("beef Stroganoff"). Some financed the 1905 and 1917 revolutions, not foreseeing that in this they would annihilate themselves. In their entrepreneurial zest and egalitarian instincts, they resembled Americans more than Russians.

My mother's Muscovite grandparents were cultured, great music lovers and operagoers. In her adolescence, my grandmother heard Anton Rubinstein, the greatest Russian pianist of the nineteenth century and in his heyday one of the world's most famous, play in Moscow. He was old then, but still a master. My grandmother had married young and widowed quickly. A young widow, she met my grandfather on a cruise on the Volga River. One day, they found themselves standing next to each other on the deck, admiring the view. Nature then took its course.

At the time of my mother's birth, Kiev was the third-largest city in Russia, with some two hundred fifty thousand inhabitants. It was by then over a thousand years old and was also Russia's original capital before the Mongolic invasions of the thirteenth century.

∾

Contrary to my grandmother's bland estimates of the course of history, little Assia was not destined for a quiet, uninteresting life. At the very moment of her birth, the nascent twentieth century was building up its lethal energies. In Russia, fevered tensions — social, economic and political — marked the decade and a half between my mother's birth and the outbreak of the First World War.

At one end, the rapid rise of an educated and increasingly prosperous middle class, the spread of Western political and cultural ideas, and rapid industrialization infused Russian life with modernist progress. At another extreme, forces of inertness — an illiterate and backward peasantry (some 80 percent of the population), a largely medieval tsarist regime abetted by the land-owning gentry, aristocracy, and the church — stood as barriers against change. At a third apex stood radical, predominantly Marxist revolutionaries. The latter saw no alternative for Russia but a violent revolution. At the intellectual and spiritual fulcrum resided the novelist Leo Tolstoy, intolerably liberal to conservatives. Unimaginable today, his almost worshipful popularity galvanized progressive opinion.

7

A geopolitical event brought the latent collisions into the open. By the beginning of the twentieth century, unheralded Japan had entered in imperialist competition with Russia in Manchuria, a Chinese province. A war followed in 1904 and Japan defeated Russia, with direct consequences on my mother's destiny. Russia's defeat, an effect of the tsarist regime's fecklessness, produced the first Russian revolution, in 1905. History now intruded upon my mother's early childhood.

> *I don't remember much before 1905 and particularly not the revolutionary events of that year. They did not affect us much in Kiev. Most of the depredations and violence took place either in rural properties, or in industrial cities like Moscow or St. Petersburg. Kiev was mostly peripheral to all that. Nevertheless, I would occasionally wake up at night that year, hearing loud bangs. It was a hired night watchman walking through our large garden, frightening bandits away. Father told us later that anti-Semitic pogroms took place at that time and that Mr. Yudelovich, the Jewish merchant who supplied us with coal and heating wood, lived in our house with his family until the threat of pogroms subsided. I wonder what happened to them and whether they escaped Kiev when the Germans arrived in 1941.*
>
> *Adults began to use incomprehensible words, "the black one hundred," "SR," "SD," "expropriator."*

The black one hundred referred to extreme, reactionary, at times violent conservatives. *SR* referred to the Socialist-Revolutionary party, very active during the 1905 revolution. Though politically less radical than the *SD*, some of its members practiced terrorism and assassinated numerous government officials. *SD* referred to the Social Democrats, the essential Marxist party in Russia. It spawned the Bolsheviks, led by Lenin. *Expropriator* described violent revolutionaries who brutally confiscated large land holdings to the presumed benefit of peasants.

The 1905 revolution exploded leaderless and spontaneous, with much murder, fury and burning of estates. Though it sprang viscerally from the long-suffering Russian peasantry and the new industrial proletariat, it also became the coming-out party of twentieth century's Marxism and other violent deformations of socialism. Surprised by the revolution's spontaneity, the Marxist parties — the Social Democrats and the Socialist Revolutionaries — tried to participate. They performed some targeted assassinations and generally rehearsed for the future. Lenin laid plans in prudent exile in Switzerland, while Trotsky experimented on the ground in Russia. Arrested, he escaped to fight another day, fatefully for Russia. The Russian state, unlike the Soviet dictatorship, was leaky and escaping was all too common.

The 1905 revolution ended inconclusively, after much violence on all parts, though for the moment weak Tsar Nicholas' government prevailed.

Throughout my childhood, my parents assigned priority to our learning foreign languages. In the early years, my brother and I had a Swiss-French governess, who taught us French. When I was five, I asked Mother, "Where does our governess go in the afternoons?" "To take courses at the Alliance Française to improve her skills in teaching French." (The Alliance Française is the French government's chain of language schools in foreign countries.) Unfathomable destiny: how could I have imagined that some fifty years later I would be the director of a branch of the Alliance Française in Argentina. How much stranger than fiction is life!

In 1906, new words again, "the San Francisco earthquake." "Is that far?" I asked Mother. "It's in America." Unfathomable destiny again: little did I know that someday I would live near San Francisco and become an American.

In 1908, an event, sensational for us, occurred in Kiev. Sergey Utochkin, a mechanic by trade I believe, declared that man could fly. I doubt that many Kievans were aware that Clément Ader had already flown an airplane in France for some fifty meters in 1897 (or that the Wright brothers had done even better in 1903). One day, Utochkin performed on the city's outskirts. An enormous crowd gathered. My parents took me and my brother to this unusual spectacle. Our coachman's hat displayed the entry ticket and we remained in our coach. I didn't see how the pilot got into his biplane, but the motor revved up and the plane rose in the air. We saw a man sitting on a little chair, and though he didn't fly very high, it seemed to us that there was an abyss under him. He circled the field twice (yes, twice!) and when he landed, the crowd roared with delight.

Of course, by 1908 air flight was fairly well established, but not in Russia. Flying progressed rapidly. In 1909, Blériot crossed the Channel. In 1913, the young Igor Sikorsky flew over Kiev in his Ilia Muromets (the world's first four-engine bomber). How could I have imagined then that I would live to witness a man on the moon in 1969!

The same Igor Sikorsky, as an émigré, became American and developed all those Sikorsky airplanes and helicopters that have contributed to the United States economy, government, and wars.

Also in 1908, a powerful earthquake devastated Messina, in Italy, while a Russian fleet was in its harbor. Our sailors rushed to help. Kievans spoke much about that at the time.

I remember well 1911. I knew that Stolypin (see below) promoted agrarian reform. A man shot him that year in a theater in Kiev, in the presence of the Tsar, and I listened to conversations about his murder. They buried him in Askold's tomb, above the Dnepr according to his will, "Bury me where I will have been killed." Askold was a semi-mythical, probably Viking figure going back to Kiev's origins in the ninth century. His "tomb" was actually a monument to historical traditions.

History could have taken a different turn. Tsar Nicholas II, weak, poorly educated and inept, could not understand the forces unleashed by the 1905 revolution. They compelled him to promise a constitution, which he could never bring himself to deliver. He attempted halfhearted reforms. In his most promising decision, he appointed Pyotr Stolypin prime minister. Stolypin was able, modern, and looking to the West, not to Russia's doleful past. He brought reforms, especially in peasant land ownership, which created him enemies on all sides. The conservatives feared him, because his reforms enfranchised the powerless, landless peasants at the expense of vast landholdings by the few. The ideological left detested him, because his reforms made Russian society more open, fair, and prosperous, and thereby undermined the case for revolution. Nicholas distrusted him, because Stolypin drove Russia from autocracy to a constitutional monarchy. Had Stolypin succeeded, a constitutional order might have stayed Nicholas' hand in 1914 when he declared the fateful war on Germany.

Stolypin fully expected that his enemies would assassinate him. It remains uncertain whether the left or the right murdered him during an operatic performance in Kiev. He was forty-nine. My grandfather often spoke of him with great admiration. Their ideas about Russia's direction coincided.

We led a cultured life in Kiev in those years. There were institutions of higher learning, excellent secondary schools, various institutes and schools. Celebrities visited us — Rachmaninov, Shaliapin, and the Moscow Art Theater, which had brought Chekhov's plays to life. The opera and Soloviev's theater were quite professional. Mother often dispatched my brother and me, with Kolya Ushakov, our close friend, to the theater. My beloved nanny chaperoned us and fed us piroshki and fruit during intermissions. Thus gradually we became acquainted with Russian and European theater. Many Kievans gained fame and not only at home: Aldanov, Horowitz, Milstein, Professor Timoshenko, Sikorsky, the painter Aleksandra Ekster, and probably others I can't remember.

Our family loved music. In his childhood and adolescence, Father studied the violin, the flute, and singing. In 1911, Mother heard the first public concert of Jascha Heifetz, who was ten. He played Mendelssohn's violin concerto. Mother worshipped Rimsky-Korsakov and traveled to Moscow to hear his operas.

My parents traveled a great deal in Europe. Father admired Richard Wagner and took Mother regularly to Munich for the Nibelungenring festival. But Father also ached about our marked backwardness relative to Western countries. He wanted to do as much as possible for Russia during his life, but history curtailed his term.

The years before 1914 were for Russia times of unprecedented blossoming in all domains.

Indeed, at the beginning of the twenty-first century, there was in St. Petersburg a nice restaurant named *1913*, "in memory of the last good year in Russian history." And Nikita Khrushchev, the communist dictator of the 1950s and '60s, recalled in his memoirs that 1914, when he was a young blue-collar worker in Kiev, had been the best year of his life. My mother's early years certainly justified such perceptions. Her upbringing was typical of the upper middle class of late Victorian Europe, though with a pronounced Russian patriotic flavor, with much interest in Russian literature, history, and music. She attended a private school. From her governesses she learned French, German, and English. My grandparents set great store by education and, in addition to the governesses, my mother and her brother had a succession of tutors to deepen their education. My mother's life in those years consisted of school and family, concerts and theater, some travel within Russia, mostly visiting family, and vacations in Belgium and on the Baltic coast, in what is now Latvia.

Like many children of educated families, my mother had a "museum," collecting odds and ends, mostly odds. So began a lifelong interest in nature: leaves, feathers, colored glass washed by the sea, strange rocks, etc. Late in life, already in America and in her seventies, after women had received increasing societal recognition, she told me that she regretted not having become a biologist; that in these early interests in nature she should have heard a calling. But that, of course, is not what Russian girls expected from life at the beginning of the twentieth century.

Russian traditions predominated in the Lapinski family. Under my grandmother's strongly religious influence there was regular churchgoing, observation of religious feasts, particularly of Lent, followed by the greatest Russian holy event, Easter. On that day, all Russians without social distinctions and even if personally unacquainted, upon meeting would kiss each on the cheeks three times saying "Christ is Risen" and in response, "Indeed he is Risen." My very busy grandfather, a religious skeptic but a Russian traditionalist, dutiful toured all their acquaintances on that day and left his card at each home, relieved in most cases if the occupants weren't there. My mother brought me up in all these traditions, though under my grandfather's unintentional, but profound intellectual influence I too grew to be a skeptic.

Father had built a sixty-room clinic in the back of our large property in Kiev and equipped it according to the highest standards of comfort and the most up-to-date scientific principles. He invented a hydrotherapy process and imported its motors and all other equipment from Germany. His clinic was considered the best of its kind in Russia at that time and he intended to create a chain of such clinics across the country. (It was the predecessor of the large hospital built later by the Soviets.)

Father always rejoiced when someone displayed initiative. Some citizens formed an association in Kiev to develop vacation destinations in the Crimea. They invited Father to their first meeting and, optimistically, he attended. The organizers seemed well-to-do, but had evidently never traveled abroad. "Let's build some huts above Yalta," they proposed. Father became disgusted, "Huts? Why Yalta needs a hotel with a thousand rooms." "Oh, no, Professor. Who needs that?" Father cooled off and never attended again. Subsequent events validated his views, as the Soviets built numerous large hotels throughout Yalta and, more generally, the Crimea.

In the years before the 1917 revolution Father wrote much, often working on his manuscripts late into the night. I recall that he published in the two journals considered the most scientifically prestigious: "Archiv für Psychiatrie und Neurokrankheiten" and "Zeitschrift für die Gesamte Neurologie und Psychiatrie," both by J. Springer, Berlin.

Father was always at the forefront of science. When hormones gained scientific interest, Professor Pavlov, the originator of Pavlovian conditioning, wrote to him from St. Petersburg and a correspondence between them began, of which Mother kept some interesting letters. Of course, these letters, as well as many other family documents, were lost when we left the house in Kiev, fleeing the Bolsheviks in 1919. Foreign scientists followed Father's work and he often received letters from European countries and from the United States.

German was then the language of science, reflecting Germany's enormous intellectual power and its protean energies across all fields of human endeavor. My grandfather spoke German, as did anyone aspiring to publish in the sciences, Theodore Roosevelt, the ornithologist, included.

Though Russia had several dozen universities, Russians increasingly perfected their studies in the West. For the sciences, German universities were preeminent and Russian scientists either completed or initiated their studies there. In fact, the University of Heidelberg became a finishing station for many young Russians. My grandfather, after completing his medical studies in Russia, deepened his knowledge of the sciences there.

The perception of Russia's backwardness at the turn of the twentieth century is correct. Nonetheless, the better-educated Russians were multilingual and open to liberal Western ideas. My grandfather belonged to that generation. He was essentially a monarchist and imperialist, and would not have considered himself liberal. But he favored an enlightened polity, probably constitutional, and thought very little of the emperor and his coterie, or of the church and what he considered parasitic churchmen.

He believed in service to and defense of his country, in the fulfillment of humanitarian aims, and in an equitable world order. His idea of Russia's future resembled Germany's constitutional monarchy of the early twentieth century. But those were dreams. World War I and the Russian Revolution lurked just around the bend. The budding influence of my grandfather's generation was tragically uprooted by the 1917 communist coup that cut short the Russian Revolution.

∽

While my mother was growing up in her confined sanctuary and her father strove to improve his world, the twentieth century's cauldron already simmered to a boil. Politics grew increasingly violent, though sporadically and on an as yet relatively small scale. Less dramatically, but more profoundly, the world was rapidly evolving in social, scientific, technological, intellectual, and artistic domains.

In Russia these changes took various forms. Revolutionary terrorism, fed by an array of intransigent ideologies, continued its nineteenth-century momentum. Assassinations of officials followed one another. The 1905 revolution shook the Tsarist regime to its very core. The proletariat, the educated, even the mute peasantry became increasingly radicalized against the regime. Stolypin and other modern influences tried to maneuver the regime into a constitutional frame. For his efforts, Stolypin was, of course, assassinated in 1911. From that day on, Russia followed its tragic path to destruction.

Amid rising prosperity and technological and scientific modernity, less visible forces also revolutionized the culture. In music, poetry, and painting, the restless, passionate young attacked and ravaged precedent and tradition, often in a deliberate intent to scandalize and to tear down. "Damned poets," Bely and Andreyev among many others, wrote incendiary poetry. Malevich, Kandinsky and others painted scandalously subversive abstractions. Stravinsky shocked Paris with *Rites of Spring*. All had a common purpose and the twentieth century's principal task: to deconstruct the world they had inherited.

My mother would spend her adult life trying to make sense of the unintelligible new cultural universe. But during her childhood and adolescence, she lived in her idyllic Kiev abode, ignorant of all these political and cultural disturbances. Thus unprepared, she met a dangerous world in her early teens.

The Great War – Life's First Lessons

In August 1914, two dozen mediocrities in Europe's chancelleries precipitated World War I, a cataclysm that swamped the world. No ideals motivated these men, but merely a desire to preserve continuance in the face of modernity's unsettling changes. Not a single statesman arose to prevent the march of irresponsible folly, either in Russia or elsewhere. The twentieth century's fierce ideologies waited under the surface to ambush much of humanity, my mother and her family among them.

History began for me in 1914. That year my early life ended. I was fourteen, my brother twelve. World War I caught us in Belgium, where Mother had discovered several years earlier a tiny seaside resort suitable for children, Wenduyne-sur-Mer. But that summer, in Sarajevo, Gavrilo Princip assassinated Archduke Franz-Ferdinand, heir to the Austrian throne. I didn't read newspapers yet, but knew that they sounded alarmed and expected war. We children listened to conversations of the adults and were aware of events. My parents decided to return immediately to Russia; war seemed unavoidable. We said good-bye to our governess and to the very kind student who tutored us every morning in dictation, mathematics, and Russian literature, even though we were both good students. Being Russian and of draft age, he returned home through England, our ally; we went through Germany, on whom Russia had just declared war.

We traveled without the usual comforts, but my brother and I, overcome with curiosity, didn't mind. Everything seemed well at first and I don't remember any signs of war mobilization in Germany. After only a short distance into Germany, the train stopped at a station and a spike-helmeted German entered and informed us, "Russia has declared war on us." Distraught, Father said, "Gott sei dank" (thank God), instead of what he really meant, "Um Gottes Willen" (for heaven's sake). Despite this, the German led Father politely to his superiors (those were times when no one had heard of Hitler yet). Clutching our luggage we followed him, descending into the basement of the station building. There, also arrested by the Germans, sat on a bench a tall, thin, homely man. Seeing Father, he beamed and they happily spoke Russian to each other. The German officer was happy too: "Now we have you identified." It turned out that the gentleman was Lev Kasso, Education minister in the Russian government, whom Father had known somewhat in Russia and whom the Germans, for some reason, suspected of being a spy.

We went on. As in a fog, I remember a night in a third-class car filled to the brim with Russian tourists returning home. The Germans kept us locked up over night and it was very hot. In the morning we found ourselves in Stetin and spent our second night in a cattle wagon, on impeccably clean straw. The Germans on the train behaved in a friendly fashion and a soldier even offered me plums. On the following day, they took us to Ruegen Island. There we found thousands of our compatriots with their luggage awaiting a ferry to neutral Sweden.

It seems unbelievable now that there was a time when one could travel across Europe without a visa. Only Russia and, I believe, Austria, required that foreigners have a passport. It cost five rubles and contained neither photographs, nor fingerprints. We would send our butler to the police station and he would return with the passports.

Soon after landing in Sweden, Father sent a reassuring telegram to his mother in Kiev. Malmö was a light, happy city, with many red geraniums in the windows and on street lampposts. With some difficulty, Father found a hotel room, albeit a large one, with a bathroom (what a pleasure!). My parents were unable to find out what was happening on the front because of the unavailability of foreign newspapers. Of foreign languages, the locals knew only Swedish (in my mother's paraphrase of Chekhov's punning and untranslatable joke).

Untranslatable because language-specific, puns cascaded from my mother's tongue throughout her life, in Russian, French, German, and Serb. As for Sweden, my mother would have reason to feel grateful to it again, many years later.

On the war fronts hardly anything went according to plans. Only Germany entered prepared militarily. All the other belligerents had variously readied for nineteenth-century wars. All suffered unexpected reverses, even the Germans, and just as unexpectedly the war became a slow, inexorable grinder of human flesh. The tsarist government, rotting at its core, threw troops into the efficient German war machine with irresponsible abandon. Ill-prepared and ill-equipped by an effete general staff, the Russians invaded East Prussia in early August 1914 to relieve pressure on the French front. The well-organized Germans, rapidly shifting their troops by a modern railway system, destroyed them. .

Of the rest of our trip I remember only a small ship and a sea so shallow that here and there appeared warning buoys. At long last, Finland (then part of the Russian empire). We got off the ship onto small wooden bridges over a swamp and then on a train of sixty cars, all third class with wooden benches. It took three days to travel to St. Petersburg. Fortunately, the day before we started the empress dowager had traveled through this area and ordered that the refugees be fed at all stations. I remember that there weren't enough forks and our adventures continued; mother became very tired. We traversed deep forests and skirted picturesque cliffs. Finally, St. Petersburg and rest.

My parents loved art and took us the following day to the Alexander III museum and after that to the Church of the Spilled Blood, where Tsar Alexander II was mortally wounded. Of course we saw the Bronze Horseman. But a square with two ancient buildings struck my adolescent imagination most vividly: the Holy Synod and the Governing Senate. Very stately and majestic.

Tsar Alexander II was assassinated by revolutionaries in 1881. The Bronze Horseman is a statue of Peter the Great, very famous in Russia. The buildings mentioned by my mother still stand, as does the Bronze Horseman facing the Neva River.

I don't remember how we traveled to Kiev, but every year when we returned from vacations familiar places had changed their appearance. And now we were especially impatient to see our nanny and our grandmother, to smell the odors of the house, and to run as fast as possible into the garden with its paths now lush and darkened in deeper shadows during our absence. With what emotion we neared the Dnepr from the east, anticipating the minute when we would sight the cupola of the Monastery of the Caves glowing in the sun, rising above the parks!

Kiev stands on a steep and lofty cliff over the Dnepr, its summit thick with stately trees in lushly green parks. Behind them looms the Monastery of the Caves, the oldest in Russia. It features a splendid, golden, eighteenth-century Baroque cupola over its tenth-century monastic caves. The monastery remains fully functioning today and the surrounding landscape has not changed since my mother's childhood.

Our voyage may have then seemed catastrophic to many, but no one could have imagined what awaited us all in the not-too-distant future. We children felt little of the war initially. The girls among us would bring packages to our gymnasium (secondary school) to be sent as gifts to soldiers on the front. The taking of Lvov was celebrated with a solemn Te Deum mass on St. Sofia square, with the attendance of all the gymnasiums.

In 1914, the Russian armies suffered crushing defeats against the Germans, but were successful against the Austrians, especially in the taking of the important city of Lvov.

That year, I began the fifth year in our Duchinskaia gymnasium and Nikita the fourth. We had both earned silver medals upon completing the preceding academic year. By 1915, lines materialized throughout the city. Though there was no lack of foodstuffs or other consumer products, it was urgent to supply the front with indispensable necessities for the troops. Refugees from Poland kept arriving in Kiev and new pupils kept appearing in our gymnasium.

Our tutor, Nikolai Grigorievich Kuznezky, had returned from Belgium through England without difficulty and was immediately drafted. On the front he lost a hand — and then his wife, whom he loved, but who abandoned him. He shot himself. That was the war's first strong impression for us children.

Troops often passed in front of our house, on their way to the railroad station. I remember the young, distressed face of Sergey, Mother's cousin, when his cavalry squadron rode to the station. Some officers returned to the sounds of a military band, as they were taken to the cemetery.

To his multiple activities, Father now added constant, of course, voluntary visits to the military hospital. Even before the war, he treated the military, the clergy, and people of limited means at no charge. Many Russian physicians probably did the same. In 1915 he gave a lecture on the "Development of personality in women," to raise funds for the troops. He was well known in all of Kiev, was a good speaker, and consequently the large university hall couldn't accommodate all those who wished to hear him. He repeated that lecture several days later.

My grandfather worked on the forefront of neuropsychiatric research in those years. Psychology also interested him, specifically the development of the female personality, then a new field of inquiry. Despite all the subsequent upheavals of his émigré life, the quasi totality of his written work — 151 scientific papers — survived and resides on my shelf. Among them, I find one, almost two hundred pages long, on the development of the female personality — no doubt the source of his lecture. It consists mostly of his own research, but also broadly references the then extant, mostly German and French, literature.

I regret to report that today's opinion would greet that lecture with dismay and maybe boos. My grandfather concludes that the physiological imperative controls women's personality development. Specifically he posits that their physiology determines women as reproducers, thereby placing limits on their ability to develop in other fields. No doubt my mother accepted these views, but that was the lot women until the invention of the pill in 1960.

> *Also in 1915, to allow him to visit his family on Sundays, Father bought a country estate called Old Balanovka, near Bucha station, not far from Kiev. It had a happily intimate house set in a park of some fifty acres. He paid fifty thousand rubles for it, though unfortunately I don't know the prices of much that surrounded us. Close by was the estate New Balanovka, belonging to the Krasovskis. We played tennis with Mitia Krasovski and became great friends. Kolya Ushakov, Mary and Kotya Voronetz, our closest friends, often came to stay. We spent three unforgettable summers there. Father also bought an orchard of over fifty acres in the Caucasus, also for fifty thousand rubles, sight unseen, having sent a trusted man. It seemed to have been a shrewd investment, because Stalin later built a dacha for himself on it.*

Mitia and Kolya were not just great friends of my mother's, but probably the first boys interested in her romantically. I find among her belongings a small, elegant album in which her secondary school friends wrote memorable sayings as keepsakes. Most are poems, a national passion among Russians. On one page, Mitia wrote, in beautiful calligraphy, my mother's nickname *Assia* in ancient Persian cuneiform, in Sanskrit, in Arabic, in ancient Hebrew, in Greek, in ancient Slavic, and in stylized Cyrillic. Not to be outdone, Kolya contributed several long poems of his own.

Meanwhile, painful for a Russian heart to recount, Russia's war prospects deteriorated catastrophically. In January and February of 1915, the Germans scored several crushing victories and in spring broke down the Russian central front. This led to a retreat toward Kiev in the summer of 1915. The fecklessly inept tsarist regime often left entire armies without rifles or ammunition, while millions of bullets and artillery shells languished where not needed. An organized, competent German state now delivered blow after blow at a Russian state undermined for centuries by the disarray of an incompetent and corrupt bureaucracy. The morale of Russian troops still mostly held, encouraged by occasional victories, mostly against Austrians and Turks. But the officer corps began to show signs of a wavering confidence — an early harbinger of the revolution to come.

> *As the war intensified, many in Kiev donated their gold to raise funds for soldiers. My dear nanny, Evdokia Zaharovna, contributed her modest earrings. We had no governess anymore, but lovely Miss Florence Pearce, our English teacher, spent each summer with us. In Kiev, in addition to English, we continued to take French and German lessons from teachers who came to our house.*
>
> *The war dominated many conversations. People rejoiced at our victories and grieved about defeats. The summer of 1915 was unsuccessful and our troops retreated. When the front approached Kiev to some five hundred kilometers (three hundred miles), panic ensued. They transferred the university to Saratov (over six hundred miles farther east). Father didn't want to leave the house, but he sent the family to the Crimea.*
>
> *Grandmother, with her maid Sasha and under the supervision of Father's assistant, Dr. Tiankin, went first. Grandmother Maria Sokotskaia lost her parents early. Komarovski, the marshal of nobility of the Chernigov gubernia, became her guardian.*

Marshals of nobility were elected individuals charged with seeing to the interests of the nobility, the only order in Russian society so advantaged. The nobility comprised great magnates, who could take care of themselves, and a large mass of hereditary gentry, most rather lazy and parasitic. That these marshals existed says much about the reasons for revolution in Russia. Gubernias were major Russian administrative units — some eighty of them. My paternal grandfather was marshal of nobility of the Ufa Gubernia.

As a young girl, Grandmother met my grandfather, Nikita Lapinski, at the Komarovskis'. Nikita was born in 1812, in a wheat field near Smolensk, as the Russian troops were retreating before Napoleon and the family house was burning in the distance. He worked in the gubernia governor's administration. Grandmother married him, but he died only a few years later. She lived to a very old age, followed all events during the Great War in the newspapers, but was lucky to die a year before the revolution.

After Grandmother, we too arrived in Yalta. Mother placed us immediately in the local gymnasium. With us arrived a student, Bogdan Andreevich Trishchenko, cultured and cheerful: he was expected to tutor us so that we could keep up with this new gymnasium. With him we hiked a great deal and he taught us botany and geology. He died in the 1920s from typhoid fever, as millions did. Our stay in Yalta was saddened by the unexplained death of our maid Marfa: she left the house one day and didn't return, but on the ninth day the sea surrendered her body.

But there were good memories as well. In the cathedral we heard for the first time the Credo, by Grechaninov, that pearl of our church music. There was a "historical" episode. One day we were on the wharf with our tutor, when we heard explosions and two columns of water rose from the sea. And immediately from behind a cape to our right two minesweepers appeared, continuing to shoot. We could see from afar that they were increasing their speed, stirring our patriotic feelings. On the prow of the first ship we could see a little flag indicating that an admiral was in command! The firing continued, but the German ship managed to escape.

The Crimea enchanted us children: the nature, the atmosphere of Yalta, charming Tartars trying to speak Russian correctly (which evidently gave great joy to my mother and her brother, who composed a poem consisting of incorrect Russian spoken by the locals). We spent some three months in the Crimea and then returned to Kiev after the situation on the front improved.

At this point in her journal, my mother quotes other puns and untranslatable poetry by her fourteen-year-old brother. They include a translation from English of a Longfellow poem. Some of Nikita's poems were darker, anticipating tragic events to come. She was very proud of him.

> *By now, it was 1916. The adults spoke about the war, about the politics in Petrograd; and rumors, many rumors. And Rasputin's death. In 1914, at the start of the war with Germany, the Russian government had renamed the city with a Russian-sounding name, Petrograd, to replace the German-sounding "Sankt Petersburg."*

In 1916, Europe's history reached a point of no return to the known past. That watershed year sowed the seeds of the world that followed, in which societal structures of all imperial and colonial powers broke down irreparably. On the Western front, as on the Eastern, millions died in vain. The two subsequent decades exposed what the slaughter did to men's hearts and souls.

Russia continued to deteriorate. The tsar, unintelligent, uneducated, lacking in character, was surrounded by venal scoundrels. The physical condition of his only son and heir, a hemophiliac, contributed much to that. Grigori Rasputin, a Siberian adventurer who passed himself off as a holy monk and something of a miracle worker, seemed to have a calming effect on the heir and particularly on his rather hysterical and superstitious mother. With his sway over the Tsar's family, Rasputin influenced Nicholas II to appoint the inept and the dishonest to positions of high responsibility.

Meanwhile the front mostly held, and, in fact, Russian victories against Austrians and Turks multiplied, but not against the Germans. General Brusilov's victorious offensive against the Austrians during that summer still produced half a million Russian deaths. Soldiers now deserted in large numbers. Some sixty thousand flooded into the cities, especially into Petrograd, where they swelled a revolutionary-minded proletariat. In December 1916, a group of officers including a grand duke relative of the Tsar assassinated Rasputin. But it was too late. The revolution lurked just around the corner.

At the very eve of the revolution took place the social highlight of my mother's life when she was introduced to the empress dowager of Russia. She treasured that memory.

In December 1916, Elena Nikolaevna Bezak, wife of the marshal of nobility of the Kiev gubernia, organized a daytime play, "Children to Children," to raise funds for war orphans. She invited me and Nikita to participate. That is how we became "actors." In emigration, Mrs. Bezak, ended her days in Berkeley, in California, living with her youngest daughter and grandson. Now she rests in the Serbian-Russian cemetery near San Francisco, where I have already bought a spot. If a fortune teller had foretold us then, in Kiev, that we would both be lying in California's soil, we would have thought her deranged.

But I digress. Two days before the performance, Mrs. Bezak took us to the palace overlooking the Dnepr, where the empress dowager resided. We children went in eight automobiles, up Aleksandrovskaia Street, passing troops returning from a Te Deum mass above the Dnepr.

After driving into the park, we entered the palace, which, being young, I didn't examine carefully. Surely, there were many wonderful things there. We went up one floor, where in a very light hall we were positioned into a half circle. The doors opened and the empress entered quietly, walking between Mrs. Bezak and Countess Ignatieva, wife of the governor. Behind them came old Admiral Shervashidze. Fourteen-year-old Mira Bezak stepped out and thanked the empress in Russian for accepting the invitation to our performance (French would be the expected language at court, but war patriotism required reverting to the vernacular). The empress walked the line of children, extending her hand to be kissed by the boys; the girls, in white or pink dresses, curtsied. In the hall next door tea was served at enormous round tables.

The performances took place on January 18-21, 1917. First, the children from the orphanage performed traditional peasant children's songs and dances. Then our group presented "The Match Making," after a text of Aleksei Tolstoy. We had all been very well prepared by local actors. Nikita played Prince Vladimir and beautiful Irina Davidova played the princess. Both wore brocade costumes in which Mr. and Mrs. Bezak had danced at a famous ball in St. Petersburg in 1903. My mother goes on to list what other numbers the children performed, including dances and songs, herself dancing a gavotte in eighteenth-century dress and a white wig. Miraculously, I have kept a picture of the whole group after the performance. Unfortunately, I burned the program during terrifying 1919.

After the performance, the empress had tea with the ladies in one of the salons and kindly addressed herself to my mother, "Comme votre fils a bien joué le vieillard" ("How well your son has played the old man"). As she rose to leave, a band played the national anthem, "God Save the Tsar." Five weeks remained before the revolution.

Two events in 1917 exceeded all others in historical consequences: the Russian revolution and the American entry into the Great War. Both determined my mother's destiny. She suffered from the first, but eventually and gratefully benefited from America's world ascendancy that began that year.

At the end of the Great War, monarchies and empires collapsed into history's dustbin. Forceful ideologies, mostly mutations of socialism, and various nationalisms now came to the fore. Socialism transmuted fearsomely into communism, Nazism and fascism. My mother's destiny unfolded under the impact of lethal men spewed forth by the collapse of the empires. In 1917, Hitler was wounded, but he lived. Had he not? Neither Lenin, nor Stalin fought in the Great War or any other. All three went on to sponsor the next chapters of my mother's life.

Revolution and Civil War — Life's Harsher Lessons

The Russian revolution burst out in Petrograd on February 23, 1917. Largely spontaneous and hence chaotic, it quickly spread throughout the country in repeated explosions of fury over repressed, centuries-old grievances, exacerbated by the sufferings brought on by the war. As in 1905, enraged peasants and soldiers lynched the well-to-do, burned their properties, and even castrated pedigree horses to punish them for belonging to the aristocracy. It reached Kiev rapidly.

> *My parents, though disapproving of the revolution, construed it as a consequence of the behavior of the feckless government in Petrograd. Their dominant concern and that of many in 1917 remained not to lose the war against the Germans.*
>
> *After "February" life changed abruptly. Everywhere around the city red posters, portraits, slogans ("Dialog with the enemy through machine guns"). Political meetings were held on street corners, army deserters lay about on the sidewalks, rudeness reigned, the*

word "burzhui" (bourgeois) became an insult. All reminders of the old regime were broken or destroyed; they even took down the statue of archangel Michael from the roof of City Hall.

These factual, descriptive lines hide deep lacerations in my mother's life, so suddenly, incomprehensibly, overturned. Initially, the February revolution zigzagged feebly, ideologically uncertain. Weak, hesitant, temporary governments, ranging from bourgeois to increasingly left, succeeded each other throughout 1917, attempting democracy against forces on the right and on the left. On the left, the communist Bolsheviks plotted and agitated to subvert the temporary government. Aleksandr Kerenski headed the last phase of the Provisional Government before the Bolshevik coup in October 1917. A member of the Social-Revolutionary party — though, in fact, rather bourgeois — Kerenski attempted opportunistic political maneuvers. He tried to keep the war against Germany going, despite massive desertions and insubordinations fomented by the Bolsheviks. He was theoretically the commander-in-chief, but was known as the exhorter-in-chief when he harangued the troops at the front, begging them to go on fighting.

In 1917, Bolshevik Vladimir Lenin entered history and through him surfaced communism, the first of the twentieth century's viral ideologies. That spring, the Germans, at war with Russia, decided to import the insidious communist virus to decompose Russia internally. They conveyed Lenin in a sealed train through Germany, out of his exile in Switzerland and into neutral Sweden. He landed in Petrograd two months after the revolution had broken out.

In Russia, where the overwhelming majority of population had a clear ethnic identity, Lenin was a cultural outlier. His ancestry mixed ethnicities to a then extraordinary degree. In addition to Russian (his real last name was Ulianov), it contained Kalmyk, Mordva, Swedish, German, and Jewish strands. He arose as a natural internationalist with no emotional commitment to a particular country.

The German ploy succeeded all too well. Upon arriving in Petrograd, Lenin conspired to undermine the Provisional Government through a series of plots. Most failed, but on October 25, 1917 Lenin launched a coup that overthrew the Provisional Government. Kerenski fled, the Bolsheviks immediately dissolved the elected Duma (Parliament), and instituted rule through terror. That ended the many proto-democratic aspirations of the Russian revolution. My mother's photo album contains pictures of the Bolshevik coup in Petrograd, clipped from newspapers.

Bolshevik terror gave rise to a civil war between the communist Reds and the Whites resisting them. It lasted some three years. The several White armies consisted of volunteers, including boys like my father and my mother's brother. Many others were military, generally officers, often serving as privates. Some belonged to the now dispossessed classes, others came from among the educated, some from the better-off peasants, and some even from among socialist factory workers. The Whites were overwhelmingly nationalist. Many hankered nostalgically for an imperial past, but most groped for a national ideology that would stem the demise of Russian national identity and religion. In diametrical ideological contrast, the Reds represented a violent mutation of international socialism, aiming to implant the Marxist Utopia in Russia. The Red armies consisted of both volunteers and conscripted workers and peasants.

Leon Trotsky, leading ideologue of communism and of rule through terror, turned out to be a capable military organizer and as such directed the war against the Whites. The Whites massed principally on three fronts: in the south, the east, and the northwest. In command of Russia's armament industry and of a central network of railroads, the Reds readily deployed their well-armed divisions from one front to another. The Whites, heavily outnumbered and often in ideological and organizational disarray, eventually succumbed.

The coming of the communist regime in Russia also pioneered another twentieth century ideological innovation — population control through institutionalized, totalitarian terror. The Bolsheviks tool was the Cheka, the first name of the communist police organizations, the eventual KGB. The Cheka admitted to shooting sixty-three hundred persons in the first year of its existence. By comparison, the tsarist regime had executed for political reasons two hundred individuals during the entire nineteenth century.

I don't remember when the civil war began for us, but I think that it was soon after "October." One day, the city found itself under artillery fire and the Reds bombarded us with rather small shells.

31

My brother and I gathered little shrapnel balls in our garden. Two shells hit the house. That which hit the roof exploded in the attic, to the detriment of the laundry that was drying there. In the garden we found a round hole in the brick wall with an unexploded shell in it. It had apparently landed there at the end of its flight. The inhabitants took refuge in basements and we hid in a halfbasement. There was no panic. It seemed more tiresome than frightening.

The Reds entered Kiev probably in early 1918. Soon rumors circulated that attacks and murders of landowners had begun in Chernigov gubernia. About Smoligovka, our former country estate (in the Chernigov gubernia and where the Lapinski family originated), or about Balanovka, only an hour from Kiev, we knew nothing. There were other things to worry about. We were horrified to learn that our closest friends, the Komarovskis, had been atrociously murdered, together with their servants. They spared only a three-year-old child with its nanny. Its father had luckily left for Chernigov on business the day before this frightening occurrence. Another neighbor, Vladimir Korostovetz, described all this in detail in "Seed and Harvest," published in London, in 1931.

That book represented a plethora of such literature by émigrés in 1920s and '30s, analyzing the root causes of the Russian revolution. My mother read many of them. Her adult life was overshadowed with the obsessive questions: What happened? Why? Many of these authors reached conclusions similar to my mother's, that the old order had needed a radical reform. By then, however, the horse had left the barn.

With the arrival of the Reds, the Cheka came into being in Kiev and terror began. It is hard to convey the population's state of anxiety and confusion when terror reigns in the city. People burned documents and buried arms. I was told of an acquaintance who went to bury his revolver in the botanical garden. As he dug a hole, he found a saber wrapped in oil cloth already buried there. The military suffered the most: searches took place during which they sought "weapons." But how can one burn or hide a uniform? During the day they looked for arms; at night they arrested. Finding an officer's shoulder boards was tantamount to a death sentence. Colonel Nikolai Vasilievich Pestov, the husband of Father's cousin, was arrested on a street and shot with other officers. They killed them the same day, it seems in the park of the empress's palace. His widow identified his body by his socks in the university's anatomic theater. Shoeless corpses were piled up like cordwood. Mother told me that at his funeral there were only two persons.

The Cheka killed to frighten. Father's popularity saved him for the time being, but we lived in fear. The Cheka had already reached into the university and shot Professors Armashevski and Florinski. The newspapers listed names of the killed as "enemies of the people." I personally saw on Timofeev Street, by the university morgue, a cart loaded with a heap of corpses. From under a tarp stuck arms and legs and one bearded head. The draft horses strode heavily. Walking one morning to my gymnasium, I passed a walled compound. From under its gates a stream of blood trickled between the cobblestones. It was the blood of those shot the night before by the Cheka. I never forgot. After I emigrated, when I would tell all this to foreigners, I realized that they didn't believe me. Not surprising!

One can get used to very much, but how not to feel profoundly indignant (silently, of course) when, during a search, a commissar, attended by two armed soldiers, digs through your cupboards and desks and takes out your personal belongings. Things of some value disappeared. Confusion reigned in the city and we expected anarchy.

After he absorbed the details of our new existence, Nikita wrote funny, sarcastic, but bitter verses commenting on the conditions. When the revolution's ravages began in 1917, the fifteen-year-old wrote this poem — like all poetry, not properly translatable:

Stars barely shine
in the twilight of heaven's vault,
while settles dewy fog.
Better there be a storm
in this sleeping nature
to fuse with the storm in the soul.

Better that lightning
would flash in the sky
that thunder would sound.

Behold: perishes Russia,
fatherland dear,
by the will of its sons.

The newspapers published galling orders. They announced a "day
of shoes," or of dresses, or of coats, meaning that the local Bolsheviks
would come around to confiscate shoes, dresses or coats. We had to
urgently prepare packages for which the "comrades" came. Nikita
(by then seventeen) and his friends Kolya and Mitia left the city and
hid in an abandoned rural dacha, waiting for the Whites to arrive,
to return to Kiev and volunteer for their army.

I don't remember whether we drove in our car anymore, but
I recall that we learned to our surprise that our chauffeur was a
communist and was spreading propaganda among our house staff.
He turned out, however, to be ineffective, as all our staff greatly
respected Father. Our butler Vassiliy sent touching letters to Father
in Zagreb after we had emigrated. We learned accidentally that our
house in Balanovka had been plundered. My nanny saw Mother's
smock on the street on an unknown woman.

Mary Voronetz was my closest friend. The commotions of the
civil war separated us and we never met again. But unknowable
fate once more: I met her brother years later, already in exile in
Belgrade, in Yugoslavia, a country that didn't exist in 1918. Now
his wife became my closest friend in Belgrade. Mary's much younger
sisters, Vera and Natasha, experienced bitter destinies. Vera died in
a Gulag camp, in Siberia. Natasha died in emigration, after her
husband was shot by the Bolsheviks.

After the Germans occupied Kiev (see below), someone knocked
on Father's study: "Come in." Before Father stood an embarrassed
chauffeur. "Mr. Professor, don't inform against me." Father didn't
hold grudges, "Go." And he didn't inform against him.

The civil war unleashed chaos across Russia in 1918 and 1919.
Numerous forces that no one suspected even existed came out of the
proverbial woodwork. They moved freely across the land, fighting each
other, not always for clear purposes. Kiev was often a strategic objective.

Kiev switched hands many times: Mahno, the Greens, the Reds, the Ukrainians. I don't remember the sequence of events. In many homes people instituted night watches. In spring of 1918, the Germans occupied Kiev (they had already signed a peace treaty with Lenin). Shortly before their arrival, the Cheka shot some five thousand people, mostly military. When the Germans arrived, many Kievans went to the Cheka basement to look for the corpses of murdered relatives. We found out then that both of Mother's brothers-in-law had been killed in different parts of Russia.

Upon their arrival, the Germans immediately instituted order and behaved correctly, but plundered the country, taking anything they wanted to Germany, as they were still at war and threatened by hunger. They also created a "Ukrainian" government, headed by Skoropadski, formerly a Russian general.

As the revolution struck, various separatist movements emerged across the Russian empire. Not only ethnically different peoples from the Caucasus and Central Asia began to assert their identities, but also the Ukraine, a heretofore nonexistent entity, emerged, led by socialist and other left-leaning intellectuals. In January 1918, these Ukrainians signed a separatist peace agreement with Germany, which recognized their government to be sited in Kiev. In return, the Germans were to protect their territory against the Bolsheviks and, not incidentally, use its resources for their war needs. During the German occupation, my mother found herself suddenly living in a foreign country — Ukraine. A new yellow and blue flag came to replace the Russian white, blue, and red. My mother's family, committed Russian patriots, were horrified at the various separatist movements, whose legitimacy they derided. On a trip to Kiev in 2004, I spoke with many people I met casually in public places. All, with one exception, spoke Russian; only one spoke Ukrainian, thereby validating my mother's perceptions.

The arrival of the Germans marked a transitory normality. My mother next recounts memories of that period, remembering little episodes, snatches of happiness, which were nothing more than normal life, but which seemed like paradise compared to what preceded and what followed. Now eighteen, she reminisces happily, realizing that every little thing had immeasurable human value.

Her memoir speaks with emotion of her last Easter in Russia, as by the following Easter, in 1919, the Bolsheviks had reoccupied Kiev, closed the churches, and persecuted and often murdered priests and monks.

Easter marks in Russia the most solemn religious occasion of the year. The profound festivity and joy of the Russian Easter service have traditionally united the Russian people in ways unfamiliar in the West. On this Easter of 1918, temporarily liberated from the communists, believers flocked to assert their spiritual identity.

Nowhere did Easter resonate more profoundly that day than in Kiev, or than in my mother's soul. By then a thousand years old, the Mother of Russian cities had been Russia's capital until the Mongol invasions of the thirteenth century. In their wake, Russians retreated north and Kiev went into decline for several centuries. My mother wrote what follows with the expectation that I would understand the full impact of that particular Easter at that particular moment of her life.

Life under the Germans began to seem more normal and no one thought that the Reds would win in the end. I remember the last Easter service. In the churches everybody awaited midnight. Exactly at midnight, the deep, powerful voice of the bell in the tower of St. Sophia cathedral sounded. From all directions, all churches in the Mother of Russian cities answered with thousands of joyful voices. Now this may sound sentimental; then it deeply agitated us.

During that "German summer" we spent our last vacation in Balanovka. I remember that we locked the house only for the night, despite it already having been plundered during the earlier Bolshevik stage. Our very dear English teacher had left for home, through Siberia in 1918, with a convoy of British citizens. Some photos survived from that summer. In one, my mother sits with two friends on a garden bench in Balanovka. On another, she stands on a tennis court with her brother and two other boys, striking a feminine pose — her last shreds of happiness. Yet another, of Miss Pierce, my mother's "very dear English teacher."

Kiev came to life. The opera, theaters, restaurants, and cinemas operated. From Petrograd, Moscow, and the northern gubernias more and more people arrived. They were hungry and hoping to gain some rest. We succeeded in rescuing from Moscow our physically helpless grandmother, Anna Kornilova, and her companion of many years, very pleasant Ekaterina Jacobs.

On Proreznaia Street an office opened to register those who wished to fight in the White Army. That was under Skoropadski's Ukrainian government and it was odd to see the "foreign" (Russian) white, blue, and red flag over their door.

Among those arriving in Kiev were the painter Aleksandra Ekster and Ilia Ehrenburg. Aleksandra Ekster, was Assia Grigorovich to my parents, who had known her since she was a child and who were friends of her family. After finishing gymnasium in Kiev, she left for Moscow, where she achieved immediate success as a painter (she sent Mother some of her charming work). In Moscow, she married Ekster (I don't know who he was) and later they moved to Kiev (I also don't know when). After his death, she lived modestly and made marvelous flowers from ostrich feathers; she wasn't beautiful, but very distinguished. In emigration she lived in Paris, frequented modernist colleagues, such as Picasso and Braque, and became a cubist of some note.

From the north also escaped writer Ilia Ehrenburg, a native Kievan. I don't quite remember when I saw him. Young literati organized an evening with him at the Berlitz school. Kolya Ushakov invited me and some other friends and we observed Ehrenburg. He was dressed elegantly, but behaved rather boorishly and smoked a pipe. The younger talents drank in his sayings. I am happy about my friend Kolya Ushakov who achieved fame as a poet even though he stayed in Russia and spent the rest of his life in the Soviet Union. Ogonëk (Soviet magazine) carried a laudatory article about him in 1988 by the famous poet Evtushenko.

My mother goes on to quote a poem that Ushakov wrote in his adolescence. Ehrenburg, a famed poet already by 1918, subsequently substantiated my mother's unfavorable impression. His principles proved elastic. After navigating several ideological positions, he returned to the Soviet Union from emigration in the West and became a major literary figure, fawning over Stalin.

The Germans occupied Kiev for some nine months. The Great War ended in November of 1918 and the Germans left Kiev late that month. The German-sponsored Ukrainian regime survived them for another month. A more populist Ukrainian movement, led by Petliura, succeeded it, to utter chaos. In early February 1919, the Bolsheviks expelled those Ukrainians and returned to Kiev, making life worse than ever.

The Reds came back in February 1919. I remember that cruelest, most frightening year with a heavy heart. A feeling dominated me to get away as far as possible, as soon as possible. I didn't even experience this during the bombings of World War II. One day, sitting in our garden I thought I heard Rimsky-Korsakov's "Bumble Bee." It was a real bumble bee singing its song next to me and I thought, "This is all beautiful, but I am ready to run — anywhere, away, away." There were new "stores" in the city. The flower store sold shoes, the stationery store, gloves. All of poor quality.

Now many robberies began around the city and one happened to us in February 1919. Its leading character was one Foma, wearing an astrakhan hat and heading a gang. He rang the bell and ran into Nikita. I don't remember the details, but I saw through a glass Nikita struggling with Foma. The bandit, who was smaller than Nikita, disengaged himself and ran to the side entrance of the house. Nikita called to our servant to lock the side door while we were all running through the house. But the bandits entered and rounded us all up under the threat of revolvers. They smashed the telephone, but fortunately Mother had time to call the police. They began to rob us, but then one of the bandits called, "Foma, the police," and the malefactors disappeared instantly. It all ended fortunately without bloodletting. Meanwhile Nikita had jumped out of a window, run through the garden and jumped over the wall onto a side street. He stayed overnight at a friend's house. Next morning, unaware of what happened to Nikita, poor Father went to the morgue to look for him.

In non-communist Russia's final spasm, the Whites expelled the Reds from Kiev on August 30, 1919, and remained there till December

19, 1919.   Then the Bolsheviks returned for the following seventy-two years.   From those days, my mother's rescued photos include a gruesome document: corpses of those shot, stacked in orderly piles in a Cheka basement, discovered by the Whites on their arrival.   Hatred of communism dominated all her perceptions the rest of her life, as it did for all who survived the communist horror of those days.   I knew many.

In August 1919, the Whites finally arrived.   Life began to acquire some orderliness.   Father gave the White Army our Mercedes-Daimler, one hundred thousand rubles, and fifteen then very valuable tires that we had hid in the garden.   Gymnasium students and recent graduates volunteered for the White Army, some even fifteen-year-old children.   Among them were Nikita, Kolya Ushakov, and Mitia Krasovski; they did not accept Kolya because of impaired health.   He remained in Russia during the Soviet years and became a noted poet.

I attended Eugene Onegin with some friends to raise funds for the White Army.   For me this was a parting event.   Not many months later, already in exile, I sat with Father in a theater in Zagreb and listened to Onegin, while we wiped our tears.   Nikita left for the White Army on September 19, 1919, on his eighteenth birthday.   It was the last time we saw him.

The civil war continued.   The Red artillery shelled us and this wearied and tired us.   Once, I think in October 1919, Kievans decided to take a break and some sixty thousand of us crossed the Dnepr into Danitza.   I joined Father and Uncle Sasha, who had arrived from St. Petersburg.   We spent a night in an empty dacha and then walked home.   On the way, we saw a corpse in an empty field.   Met many acquaintances.

Kiev was changing.   There was hardly any traffic and grass grew between the cobblestones on the streets.   A depressed mood reigned: what will happen hence?   We lived quietly and saw only the closest of our acquaintances.   Mother had ceased to play four-hand piano.   Our concerns focused instead on the fate of Nikita and on the destruction of Russia.   From those days, a photo survives of my mother, now nineteen, in a White Army nurse's uniform during the Whites final stand in Kiev.

Kievans began to abandon the city. The local Polish community leased a train to Sebastopol and invited Father to come with them to the Crimea. (Poland by this time had become an independent country again and the Crimea was still in White hands.) Father hesitated, but at night the shooting resumed and he decided that we should travel to the Crimea "to take a rest from the bombings." On November 21, 1919, the day of his saint's celebration, otherwise so memorable to me since my childhood for its festive atmosphere, we began urgent preparations. Mother ordered us to pack as much warm clothing as possible and filled two suitcases as though we were leaving on a holiday in the countryside. If we had known that we were leaving forever, we would have packed differently, but that possibility didn't even cross our minds — or that Father would eventually be buried in Argentina, or Mother in Yugoslavia, an as yet nonexistent country. I did, however, take my photos with me: of my childhood home, of Balanovka, a few others.

Father gave Uncle Sasha Andriashev full powers over the management of our large house and the clinic. We traveled to Sebastopol for nineteen days. I only remember endless fields and sparkling snow. Nineteen days. The distance between Kiev and Sebastopol is less than five hundred miles. How reminiscent of the movie Doctor Zhivago, with Omar Sharif and Julie Christie!

In Sebastopol we felt the civil war even more than in Kiev, it seemed to me. I remember cavalry officers in field uniforms contrasting with colorful regimental hats. Anxiety dominated my feelings. Father rented a large room in an admiral's house. We lived in it until we left for foreign lands, leaving Russia, as it turned out, forever. The civil war was ending. In December 1919 the Bolsheviks took Kiev for a final time. This is what Roman Gul', in I Carried Russia with Me, said about those times:

Schools in Kiev were without teachers, hospitals without medications, houses without heating, stores without merchandise; the population had bread coupons, but there was no bread. People living in buildings of several stories lined up in the courtyards before the only working faucet to obtain a little water. They cut trees in Kiev's gardens and parks for wood. Exhausted by hunger, terror, epidemics, Kiev became a grand commune of beggars. The life of these beggars was governed by decrees, mandates, orders, mobilizations, confiscations, expulsions, and executions. Listings of those shot "in accordance with Red terror" were printed in the organ of the Cheka, "Red Sword," a news rag never heretofore known to the world. Chekists threatened any resistance with an increase in terror.

In early 1920, my parents decided to leave Russia when they learned that Nikita succumbed to typhoid fever. He was buried in Stavropol' without us. The cemetery was later turned into a park. That wound in my mother's soul never healed — to have lost her beloved brother, in these circumstances, and not even be able to visit his grave. Mitia Krasovski, who had also volunteered in the White Army, died similarly of typhus in Rostov at that time. He was a very dear friend of my mother's and I suspect that he harbored feelings for her.

On February 21, 1920, our small ship left Sebastopol in the fading daylight. Many passengers came to the stern. The line of land to the east grew thinner. We wept.

The White armies didn't survive much longer. Those remaining evacuated Russia through Sebastopol later in 1920, my father, my mother's future husband, among them.

Exile

My mother's sparse words don't begin to convey her despair. Her adored brother dead, her cherished house in hostile hands — she never saw it again — her country lost, her remaining family now refugees. The ship that carried them from Russia first stopped at a Rumanian port, then left them off in Varna, in Bulgaria. On that cold February day, they stepped into a bleak, impoverished, defeated Balkan backwater.

> *So we were in emigration now — refugees, not tourists, but not yet aware of our condition.*
>
> *I contracted fever and pneumonia. We stayed in Varna and spent a first night in a shabby hotel, after which Father managed to find a small room with a pleasant couple of elderly Armenians. We spent six weeks there, until I became healthy again. I don't remember the city.*

Throughout her life, my mother described her condition as "emigration" — there was Russia and there was emigration. At first and for many years, she and most Whites couldn't conceive that they wouldn't return to Russia. Surely, the monstrous Soviet regime couldn't endure.

My mother and her parents landed into a staggering world, unimaginable less than six years earlier. The Russian empire, as well as the German, Austro-Hungarian, and Ottoman, had ceased to exist. Many new national entities came to replace them.

43

In Russia, a civil war of unspeakable inhumanity was coming to an end. Throughout Europe, victors and vanquished alike had sunk to their knees, hungry, pauperized, and exhausted, racked by internal strife, reeling under the incomprehensible. The Great War had left twenty-one million physically wounded survivors. Uncounted millions more, injured in mind and soul, struggled with exhaustion and uncertainty. As a child in the 1930s, I took for normal the ubiquitousness of armless, sightless, legless men on the streets of Belgrade or on those of France.

Going through my mother's photo albums, I see her, my grandfather, and my grandmother in 1921, the first year of exile: serious, tragedy-tinged countenances, grieving eyes. What a contrast to the obligatory smiles in present-day American photos!

> *From Varna and after I became well, my parents decided to move on to Prague for reasons I don't remember. We traveled in a second-class compartment, without sleeper berths. In Bulgaria, we saw beautiful mountains, with blossoming almond trees here and there, but with often denuded mountains. They told us that enemy troops had cut down the trees during the war. The country gave a general impression of having suffered. In Sofia, I remember the Russian cathedral and in front of it the monument to (Russian emperor) Alexander II. Recent American tourists tell me that fresh flowers lay at its foot every morning and also that the population complains about the difficult life.* My mother wrote this in the 1980s, remembering that Bulgarians admired Russia in the past.
>
> *We needed travel documents and Father received them from our former consulate. These papers, called the "Nansen passport" were issued to Russian émigrés, but no country recognized their validity, which caused many problems.*

The League of Nations issued by Nansen Passports and theoretically fifty-two countries honored them, but not so in practice, as much of my mother's life was to prove. For some thirty years it was the only identification she possessed. It posed a high hurdle to overcome anytime she needed to obtain visas to travel or simply to prove who she was. Vladimir Nabokov, in *Pnin*, said this about it: "... that miserable thing, the Nansen Passport, a kind of parolee's card issued to Russian émigrés ..."

We traveled uneventfully. At the border between Bulgaria and Serbia, a young Serbian officer, on discovering that we were Russians, quickly bowed and kissed Father's hand and Father embraced him as a Serbian brother. Before 1914, the Russian government provided scholarships for young Serbs. They studied in military academies and upon graduating most returned to Serbia. They spoke Russian well and had become Russophiles. The king, then heir to the throne, graduated from the most prestigious Russian military academy. The mutual affection between Serbs and Russians remains a leitmotiv of international politics into the twenty-first century.

We stopped in Belgrade and climbed on foot to the city's center. Of Teraziya, the main square, we saw only a mound of stones. Only Hotel Moskva had miraculously survived. I am ashamed of the Austrians (who had bombed Belgrade to smithereens in 1914).

When the wave of our compatriots who had suffered from the wars landed in Yugoslavia, its king Peter immediately responded to the needs of the Russians. He instituted an exchange system: for our, by then worthless, rubles banks exchanged Yugoslav dinars. That saved many old people from hunger. Life, especially in the provinces, was cheap. When the rubles ran out, assistance continued. With the Yugoslav government's help, a Russian House was built in the garden of the former Russian embassy, with a secondary school, a library, a theater, and social services. (At that library, I read dozens of books as a child.) Most émigrés quickly adapted.

Our next major stop was Zagreb, the former Austrian Agram, in Croatia. Here a railroad strike caught us and our train sat at the station for ten days. Father and I acquainted ourselves with the city, while Mother hardly ever left the train compartment during those days. Father took me to hear Eugene Onegin at the local opera house. They sang in Croatian. We sat high up, in the cheapest seats, and wiped tears.

Zagreb turned out to be a charming, modest-sized city. It was the first along our route that was untouched by the war. We thought it truly European—no longer Middle Eastern (unmarked, as the rest of the Balkans, by centuries of Ottoman domination). Its surroundings reminded me of typical Austrian provincial landscapes. I cannot forget the marvelous aroma of alpine cyclamen there. Here our eventual destiny was decided.

On the train we made the acquaintance of a Czech doctor and we conversed with him in German, "the common pan-Slavic language." He was visiting Zagreb, or more precisely its university. From him, the university leaders found out that Father was in town. They sent a delegation of professors, who offered him a chair in his field at the new medical school, then being started. Father inquired whether they planned to have a hydrotherapy facility. "Oh, of course," they said. Father promised an answer.

The strike ended and we arrived in Czechoslovakia. There, they offered Father a chair as well, but without a hydrotherapy facility and he decided to accept the offer in Zagreb, in new Yugoslavia. Prague was an ancient, quiet, beautiful, and interesting city, but we weren't up to tourism. Our sorrowful thoughts were on Nikita and on the fate of Russia. What destiny awaits us? I could not shed the feeling that people lived around us, but that we didn't live and only observed. My parents went about depressed and physically exhausted, and decided to spend some time in Carlsbad (now Karlovy Vary, famous, as then, for its mineral springs) to regain some health. I also took baths there and drank the water. Upon moving to Yugoslavia, we continued a similar cure at Rogatska Slatina, in Slovenia.

Time was passing and two years elapsed unhappily. When I first laughed, the muscles of my face hurt. I am trying to narrate concisely our lives during those years, but it is difficult at times. This was the beginning of the period between the first and second world wars and we émigrés took no part in the world events of those times.

Through emotional exhaustion and political impotence, Russian émigrés thus remained at the margin of world events. But the fallout from the Great War generated an eruption of ideological effervescence. In devastated countries, noxious ideologies began their gangrenous march, paving the road to the Second World War. As they gained momentum, they would swallow some of these émigrés, while scalding many. Some landed in Hitler's concentration camps, others mistakenly returned to the Soviet Union to fates even worse.

Father, then, accepted the appointment in Zagreb with the hydrotherapy facility attached to the clinic, but there was such a shortage of apartments in Zagreb that we spent the winter in Vienna. Father began taking lessons in Croatian language and ordered all the equipment for the new Zagreb clinic. To his indignation ("This is what we have come to"), the German company from which he ordered the equipment wanted to give him its most expensive office set — the customary, universal petty bribing of physicians. Probably hiding his feeling, he bought instead a modest desk and other appurtenances.

Vienna had lost its ebullience, but it was still easy to imagine her splendid heyday. Even in her troubles, she enchanted. My parents encouraged my interest in Austrian culture and I often attended symphonic concerts and the Burgtheater; once Richard Strauss conducted. I would come home late — order and peace reigned in the city.

This subdued Vienna also reflected the conditions of the new Austria, reduced in the war's aftermath to one-fifth of the prewar Austro-Hungarian Empire. Vienna had been an imperial capital, waltzing to Johann Strauss. Now it was the principal city of a self-despising little republic.

We lived a retiring life, but attended the Orthodox church, in which Russian émigrés already began to appear. Father rented two rooms in a very modest pension, where we were fed accordingly. We spent our sad evenings in my parents' room. We read, we reminisced, but about Nikita we barely spoke — too painful. We mourned silently. It became noticeable later that most émigrés hardly ever remembered material losses, often quite substantial — each family had cause for genuine grief.

On New Year's Eve, December 31, 1920, we went to the movies. I have kept the program. An elderly, apparently popular, singer sang about Vienna of yore and ended, "Your shining days are past, but I remain faithful to Vienna of old." Spectators were blowing their noses. This vignette encapsulates much of Europe in the early 1920s. The world had collapsed; only memories remained for the survivors of the Great War.

Mother began to correspond with her sister who had remained in Russia. From her sister's postcards we found out about all the misfortunes that had befallen our family and probably all of Russia. She also wrote that one relative had married "an engineer from the Urals," and that another had married a man twenty years older than she. No names were mentioned and contacts are lost forever. Later, I too corresponded with cousins in Russia, but they asked me not to write.

In the early 1920s, Lenin, unsure of his grip on power, relaxed some strictures of the dictatorship of the proletariat. But by the mid-1920s, any contacts with émigrés branded one as a potential enemy of the Soviet state with potentially lethal consequences.

Thus, in April 1921 we returned to Zagreb, into a large, but uncomfortable apartment. From our windows we overlooked the city's main square, with its monument to Ban Jela i and each morning there was a market with peasant women selling the produce in their picturesque dresses.

Jela i was a nineteenth-century Croat patriot and Austrian aristocrat. In his monument my mother witnessed an early symbol of things to come. Croats never lost a sense of their national identity, tied to Austria and the Catholic West. They were now submerged in an alien entity — Yugoslavia, dominated by Orthodox Serbs, with whom they had little culturally in common except their language. Decades later this unnatural association overflowed in blood. This too affected my mother's life, as Yugoslavia split in fratricide during the Second World War.

We began to adapt ourselves to a new and alien life. Mother insisted that I continue to take piano lessons. I eventually graduated from the Zagreb conservatory. (Obedient daughter that she was, she endured the conservatory, but never played the piano thereafter. Her calling lay elsewhere, as she would acknowledge late in life.) Gradually, we began to make new acquaintances and friends, but my soul remained in Kiev. There were relatively few Russian émigrés in Zagreb — most had settled in Belgrade. Several Russian professors found positions at the Zagreb University, including Professor Saltykov, with whom we became friends. He had a scientific mind, but knew well and appreciated music, had a fine sense of humor, and was widely cultured (though twice her age, he became my mother's early, if platonic flame).

I am sure that Father found this new life constraining and boring after his intense activities in Russia. He continued to write for the same German scientific journals and corresponded with Alzheimer and other leading neuropathologists of the day. Inflation raged in Germany and the journals began to limit their pages, but from Father they accepted articles without limiting their length. Contributing to his boredom was the officialdom's inability, through lack of funds, to implement the promised hydrotherapy facility, the very reason for his choosing Zagreb.

In Zagreb we began to receive letters from Kiev, from Uncle Sasha, mailed generally from different cities. Uncle Sasha had traveled to St. Petersburg to save what had remained of his library and other property. He was still tolerated in our house in Kiev, but the day came when he, his wife, and our unfortunate nanny were forced to leave; happily, nanny found a position with another family's children. Among my mother's papers, I find a letter written from Russia by that nanny in 1925. The last link with Russia, from then forever broken.

We didn't know the details about the plunder of our house. My parents didn't even show any interest in that. I found out that Father's Zeiss microscope came into the possession of a local doctor. The pillaging didn't occur immediately upon our leaving Kiev. Apparently, the hypnotic will-power of my father still had its effect on local opinion. It is possible to imagine a forest fire, or the sinking of the Titanic, but how to imagine the unimaginable — the destruction of one's natal home? Did a drunken mob just break in and pass our belongings from hand to hand? Or did they simply drive up to the front porch and bring things out carefully and place them on hay under the new owner's severe eye, "the painting...careful?" "and where is the blue vase, and what about the blankets?" Absolutely everything was taken from the twenty rooms. I don't know about the clinic and my parents showed no interest in finding out. Probably such plundering went on throughout Russia under the Bolshevik slogan "plunder what has been plundered."

We lived quietly in Zagreb and our new acquaintances were Russians. I married Alexandr Alexandrovich Kugushev (in 1926).

This cryptic sentence describes my mother's state of mind. For most women, the act of marriage constituted the major event of their lives. She barely mentions it, but dwells in some detail on the plunder of her house in Kiev. During my life with her, I witnessed her soul as a constantly bleeding wound, never healed. She missed out on life, as did millions, traumatized by the Bolshevik effects of the Russian revolution. I doubt that her marriage was an act of profound love. It was more a meeting of two afflicted souls, in his case perhaps shattered.

My father, by all accounts, intelligent and well educated, embodied the fate of many of his generation and background. At nineteen, he and his father, then fifty-six, escaped the Red terror in St. Petersburg and made their way south through chaotic civil war Russia, to join the Whites. My grandfather soon died from typhus in a military hospital. My father, after a privileged, aristocratic upbringing and no life experience, joined a cavalry division consisting mostly of Muslim Tartars, veterans of four years of World War I. Having volunteered as a private, he fought for three years on horseback, became a sergeant and then a lieutenant. In these three formative years he learned about life, forged combat comradeships and witnessed unutterable cruelties and barbarous events. Then he fled Russia on one of the last ships out of Sebastopol with a tattered uniform and a bullet through both legs.

He landed unhinged into a convulsed, unsettled Europe and probably never found his bearings. Like many other Whites, he moved on to Yugoslavia. In Zagreb he attended the university, and met and married my mother in 1926. They moved immediately to the south of France, where they started a poultry farm, for want of a better idea. Many Whites migrated to France in those days, partly because the educated already knew French and partly because, as a former ally, France felt some obligation to receive them. For many, France represented a beacon of civilized sophistication. Photos of my father in those years show him grave, unsmiling, with joyless eyes. No smiles, no joy, either, in my parents' formal betrothal pictures. Minimal pictures of their wedding exist.

After some time (actually shortly after their wedding, in 1926), we decided to settle "on the land" in the south of France, as many of our compatriots had. On our way, we spent some time in Paris. In the 1920s, some one hundred thousand Russians had settled there. Most lived in poverty. The women sewed, the men drove taxis, or worked as waiters in restaurants. Some left for other continents. But most also began to replicate semblances of their homeland life. Throughout the 1920s, Paris became the home of Russian writers, artists, musicians, and physicians. It also housed the headquarters of White Movement Military's organization in exile, consisting of White officers who had survived the civil war. The émigrés also built a retirement home for the elderly. Various Russian associations organized balls, which produced some income. On one such evening, we saw General Kutepov in full uniform. He projected great dignity.

General Kutepov was the commander of the White Army in exile, subsequently kidnapped and murdered by the Soviets. My mother goes on to discuss Russian émigré life in Paris in the 1920s, that Paris so romanticized by Americans like Hemingway and Fitzgerald. She names the many notable Russian scientists, authors, intellectuals, and artists then living there. She notes with pride the low criminality among Russian émigrés — the French police reporting 1-1.5 percent criminality among Russians — and attributes the émigrés' moral character to their high educational standards and to the traditions of honor of the White Army. In fact, the majority of those Whites in France consisted of rank and file soldiers, unacquainted with French, or exposed to much education. My mother, with her often linguistic-based humor, drew amusement from their stumbles with the French language, which yielded a rich crop of malapropisms in French.

Upon moving to the south of France, my father purchased a farm in the Provence hinterland, not far from Nice and the French Riviera. The Riviera attracted many Russians, some notable, among whom was Ivan Bunin. He became a neighbor and friend of my parents and went on to receive the 1933 Nobel Prize in literature.

Having started his poultry farm, my husband began working with enthusiasm. His hens constantly won first prizes at farm shows in

Nice. On the Riviera we came into contact with a new and often interesting universe. We often met with the Bunins. Their circle consisted almost exclusively of literary figures, but also of aspiring writers. Rachmaninov was a friend of Bunin's and we met him there.

My mother's photo albums of the 1920s preserve episodes of her new life in the Provence with her husband. They suggest normality beginning to reassert itself: the farmhouse with a tile roof, grapevines climbing its walls and its terrace, olive and lemon trees, a square well covered by a trellis, the hen coops; my father and some French workers building a garage next to the farmhouse for his first car, a Citroen; group photos with numerous friends on the house's terrace; of relatives visiting from other parts of France, of my grandparents visiting from Yugoslavia; a group photo at a party: my father actually laughing, moderately. And in all photos the sun of southern France.

Meanwhile, Father retired in 1931 from the University in Zagreb and moved to Belgrade, where a large Russian community had rapidly formed since the beginning of emigration. Many consisted of families that had succeeded in evacuating from Odessa or the Crimea, but mainly they were the remainders of the White Army. Former soldiers and officers found themselves without financial resources. Many began to work in mines, some found modest employment in Belgrade, a few pursued university studies. Gradually, the more enterprising left for other countries where they accepted what work was available. In Belgrade there were foreign embassies, and Russians who knew languages found employment there, though of course only a few did.

By the 1930s, life in Belgrade had become good for Russians; many even became rich. It was a cozy, provincial life: family celebrations, Russian dishes, evenings playing bridge. From the ruins left by the Great War, a new city had arisen. When I visited Belgrade in 1924, the city was being rebuilt and had become unrecognizable compared to 1920. Asphalt now flooded the streets, new trees were being planted, multistory houses were being built; many stores and restaurants. By 1930, parts of Kalemegdan, the old Turkish fortress, had acquired tennis courts. A small museum there displayed the uniform in which King Alexander was assassinated in 1933 and a monumental statue by Meštrovi , the great Croat sculptor, commemorated Serbian victory in the Great War.

Serbia, the Great War's original trigger, emerged as a major beneficiary of the Versailles Peace Treaty of 1919. Austria had thoroughly devastated it during the war and Serbia lost almost 17 percent of its population, military and civilians. (By comparison, France lost 4.3 percent, both military and civilians, the United States lost 0.01 percent, all military.) As an eventual victorious ally, the Serbian king stood at Wilson's elbow at the Versailles Treaty tracing the map of a new country that became Yugoslavia. It contained, in addition to Greek-Orthodox Serbia, Montenegro, and Macedonia, Catholic and Austria-oriented Slovenia and Croatia, Muslim Bosnia and mixed Herzegovina. Though Slavs all, speaking an essentially common language, they had little in common culturally, as events in the 1990s would demonstrate.

Russian émigré families, who had cooped up in one room in the early 1920s, lived by now in normal apartments. During summers, they vacationed at resorts. Many, if not all, felt patriotic towards Belgrade and Yugoslavia.

But while these Russians dwelt unwary in their provincial Yugoslav cocoon the wheels of history began to accelerate, careening toward the century's second Armageddon.

- My mother's parents, early in their marriage.

- My mother, age ten, and her brother, eight, smiling, holding each other affectionately during a vacation on the Baltic in 1910. No premonitions of their destinies.

- *Mother's beloved house in Kiev.*

- My mother, age fifteen, in dress uniform of her school in Yalta, while her family evacuated Kiev in the face the German offensive.

- …and four years later as a volunteer nurse in the White Army

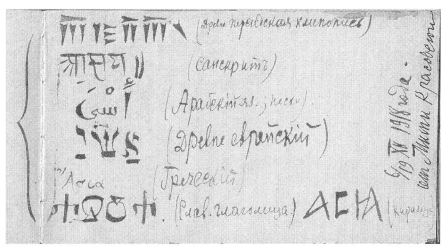

- My mother's nickname Assia in ancient Persian cuneiform, in Sanskrit, in Arabic, in ancient Hebrew, in Greek, in ancient Slavic, and in stylized Cyrillic, by her friend Mitia Krasovsky.

*- My mother's especially cherished photo of a fund-raiser
in early 1917, just weeks before the revolution. She stands,
eyes downcast, behind Russia's empress dowager.*

- November 1918, with her brother, now full of premonitions.
He will die in fourteen months; she would be exiled in fifteen.

- My mother's father, in exile in 1920. No joy.

- My twenty-one year old father as a sergeant in the White Army

- … and age twenty-three, in exile. No joy.

- My mother in her French school in Punta Chica, Argentina, circa 1958

At the
Whirlpool's Edge

The 1930s brought personal tragedy, profound changes and deepening apprehensions about the future into my mother's life. Her memoir turns cryptic.

> *Now began the 1930s. Our son Alexander was born in 1931. Mother died later that year, in Belgrade, and my husband in 1935, in France. I rented our farm to a Frenchman and returned to Father in Belgrade, with my tiny son. Father received us cordially, as always, even though we inconvenienced him, of course, in the small apartment. He appeared sad, he ailed and had aged.*

These perfunctory sentences summarize the nine years of my mother's marriage, from 1926 to 1935. My father didn't just "die," he shot himself. My mother rightly believed that by this act he had deserted her and alludes to his death in passing. In fact, it was a life-course changing event for her and for me.

My mother's photo albums contain numerous pictures of her existence in those nine years. They tell more than the scarce words in her memoir. We see an active and successful poultry farm, on which my father worked effectively and apparently enthusiastically. His Leghorn hens won top prizes at agricultural exhibitions and he earned other awards. We see him fit and lean, mowing a field with his scythe, preparing hay. He drove his eggs to Nice every morning in his Citroen.

Numerous photos focus on the first four years of my life, with my parents and with my grandparents visiting from Yugoslavia. My father holding me lovingly. Myself hugging dogs, even riding a big dog. My mother instilled in me love of dogs and several have surrounded me since my birth. Other pictures show a great variety of guests at our house. They suggest a well-rounded, warm social life in which my mother often smiles and appears socially engaged. A normal family existence emerges, passed over in pained silence in my mother's memoir.

But a fatal disease of the soul gnawed at my father. When I was a child, my mother didn't explain to me his death and I didn't think of questioning her further. In my teens, she told me how he died and I came to ask myself why my father would put a bullet through his head, with my picture on his breast. I concluded that men don't hold up to tragic change as well as women do. My mother grit her teeth and dealt with destiny as she received it, with a disciplined, determined sense of duty to me, her child. But she lacked gifts of insight into the human heart and soul, and couldn't comprehend my father in his spiritual agony.

I observed many a Russian émigré woman dealing with her tragic fate with equal courage. Men, on the other hand and across cultures, seem more prone to cave in. Their self-concept depends too often on their social circumstances. My father, brought up to serve his country, not only lost that country, but, with it, all outward marks of identity. I observed other Russian men, who, like him, had fought in the civil war, never adapting to exile, some giving in to drink and to self-pity, a fate common to political exiles.

Famous Russian composer Sergey Prokofiev had emigrated to Paris in the wake of the Bolshevik takeover of Russia. My father met him in 1927, when Prokofiev had decided to return home. My father grew indignant and couldn't understand how one could return to the communist state. Yet Prokofiev returned and endured the terror, the humiliations, and the thought control of the Soviet regime, but it was on his native soil. In the final analysis, neither Prokofiev nor my father could exist in exile.

What happens to men's souls when torn from their homeland? What happens to the souls of slaves? What happens to souls under state-imposed terror?

∽

In the 1930s the world cauldron began to boil, scalding many millions. On the path to World War II, violent men rose to power, democracies faltered and collapsed. Russia had become the terror-frozen Soviet Union. Yugoslavia's political fabric, sewn together at the Versailles Treaty under Serbian tutelage, began to come apart at its cultural seams. Reflecting the age's violence, a Croat nationalist assassinated Yugoslav king Alexander I during a state visit in France in 1933. All threads of the 1930s wove into one lethal net that changed my mother's life and mine.

The 1930s also inaugurated many innovations in human perversity. The Soviets and the Nazis installed massive, deadly concentration camps, selecting their victims by new ideological criteria. Bombing of civilian populations began in that decade. The Japanese bombed Shanghai and Nanking indiscriminately; the Italians showered defenseless Ethiopian towns with bombs; so did both sides in the Spanish civil war. My mother and I would experience a full dose of this latter innovation during the Second World War.

In the wake of her painful resettling in Belgrade, she wrote:

Our life in Belgrade turned melancholy. We made acquaintances, but the Russian community was on the whole unremarkable. After life in the French countryside, I also found the city pace difficult. I placed my son into the German school to instill discipline and to learn languages, but he also began to grow up on the asphalt streets of Belgrade.

But I also shared family life with my mother and my grandfather. Dinner conversations between them revolved around reminiscences of Russia, glorious as it was in their memories. My childhood was suffused with stories about their Russian life, about its history, literature, and music. Pushkin, Lermontov, Gogol, Mussorgsky, Balakirev and Rimsky-Korsakov held sway. My grandfather remained blissfully indifferent to all the deconstruction efforts of the artists, poets, and musicians in the early twentieth century, Stravinsky, Kandinsky, and such. My mother, while aware of all the new trends, found them puzzling.

I listened to them with increasingly mixed feelings. My grandfather marked me deeply through the sheer force of his personality. But while he and his daughter, my mother, cherished their past, I felt that it had no pertinence to my life. I was not in exile and my future lay in the West.

Pictures in my mother's photo albums show signs of recovery in her life in Belgrade during the short years remaining before the Second World War. Though in her diary she speaks of a melancholy life, images of normality appear. She vacations on the Adriatic Sea and in the mountains of Slovenia. Discrete photos too in the company of men. Walking with six- or seven-year-old me to my school; with me, again, visiting the zoo in Belgrade; with me in Venice and in Milan, while traveling to France in 1938. But hardly any photos of a social life, while she had kept so many of her existence on our farm in France.

In the late 1930s, adult White Russians around me discussed Stalin's murderous reign in the Soviet Union. The criminal massive hunger in the early 1930s, which killed millions of peasants, the arbitrary terror beginning in 1936, in which the NKVD murdered so many totally innocent people. The hunger, we found out after the war, was orchestrated by the communists to force peasants into collective farms and thus deprive them of their ownership. The knowledge of these goingson fortified our shared hatred of communists, who continued to enslave and destroy the Russia of our attachments. This also determined most of our individual decisions as World War II developed.

Meanwhile foreign newspapers spoke about the possibility of a war. Hitler rose.

In Belgrade, too, much talk of a possible war surrounded us, though that war finally reached Yugoslavia in 1941. On January 25, 1938, we celebrated the saint's day of my friend Tatiana Voronetz. Some ten of us, her closest friends, gathered for the evening. As we came out on the street at 2:00 a.m., we saw a red light flooding a lowering, densely clouded sky. We speculated that it didn't look like the glow of a fire, "Perhaps a neon light reflection." In the morning we found out that an aurora borealis, a rarest event in the

Balkans, appeared over all of Europe. People immediately began to remember the prophesy of Our Lady of Fatima (a miraculous Catholic apparition in Portugal in 1917), "After such a light there will be war." Needless to say, Europeans breathed a sigh of relief after "Munich."

My mother refers, of course, to the September 1938 conference in Munich between Hitler and the eventual allies. Hitler had ratcheted up tensions throughout Europe. After remilitarizing the Rhineland in 1936, to puny British and French protests, he now threatened Czechoslovakia. The conference convened in the democracies' hope of defusing tensions. As a boy, I remember how Munich dominated all conversations among adults in peripheral Yugoslavia. Europeans by then understood that a menace hung over the entire world, though most Americans would have perhaps felt immune. The conclusion of the Munich conference between blustering Hitler, self-satisfied Mussolini, and frightened British and French prime ministers, Chamberlain and Daladier, seemed, to the naïve, to have removed the threat of war. The French and the British thought to have saved themselves by sacrificing Czechoslovakia. Hitler remained insatiable and Poland soon topped his list.

In frantic courtship, British and French statesmen, committed by treaties to protect Poland, tried to entice the Soviet Union into an alliance to prevent Germany from invading Poland. A pact would have required Soviet troops to enter Poland on their way to fighting the Germans — capitalism inviting the communist fox into the hen coop. Poland categorically refused, understanding that once the Soviets arrived, they would never leave and Poland would disappear as a nation.

On August 23, 1939, a week before starting World War II, Germany dramatically signed a nonaggression pact with the Soviet Union. Lightning struck the adults around me. They spoke of it in total amazement: how could these ideologically and geopolitically irreconcilable foes, just recently locked in mortal combat in civil-war Spain, come to this incomprehensible alliance? In jettisoning their public ideologies, both totalitarian governments had simply reverted to the atavistic instincts of imperialism. Secretly, they divided Poland and the Baltic countries: the Soviets would receive the eastern third

71

of Poland, and Estonia, and Latvia. The Germans would keep the rest of Poland and Lithuania. Traditional Russian imperialist impulses overrode communist internationalism. Stalin, the Georgian, acted now as a Russian imperialist. German colonialist ambitions followed those of imperial Germany before World War I.

My mother was a still-youngish widow in the 1930s and men hovered. One was Mr. Pogoretzki, also a White Russian. My mother dithered about marrying him. By 1939, he probably ran out of patience with her and, believing that war was imminent, he announced that he wasn't disposed to experience it in Europe. He therefore decided to migrate as far as possible, to Argentina. This episode would have further consequences on my mother's life and mine.

> *In April 1939, I traveled to the Provence, seeking a new renter for our French property. Rumors about the forthcoming war were so insistent that I became very nervous and hurried to return home to Belgrade before they closed the borders. I found a renter through acquaintances after having already returned to Belgrade.*
>
> *September 1, 1939. After all the rumors about the possibility of war and under general nervous tension, the radio communicates the first military actions between Germany and Poland. In other words, war, though not yet a world war. But it has begun! Nerves are tense, dreadful perspectives loom. The future is so uncertain and dark that one can only pray. There is talk of a European war. In my diary that day, I note "It looks ugly. What if the war turns south?" But I am loath to comment further on historical events in my diary for fear of what may come.*

Now the 1930s preliminaries had come to an end and, as Mr. Pogoretzki foresaw, the world returned to the serious business of killing millions of human beings. Hitler got it under way. France and Britain retaliated by declaring war on Germany, as it proceeded to conquer several smaller European countries, concluding with France in 1940 and isolating Britain.

> *December 16, 1939. Events are such that the stomach churns when listening to the radio. I decided not to write about politics in my diary in case the Germans were to occupy Yugoslavia.*

March, 4, 1940. Everything around the world is very frightening. I don't want to reflect about it.

Spring 1941. On a streetcar I overheard a conversation between two elderly Serbs about politics, the Serbs' favorite topic of conversation:

- What will happen now?

- We will enter the war against the Germans, then America will come in on our side, and then it's the end of Hitler. (How prescient!)

Before the Germans occupied Yugoslavia in 1941, I began to give French lessons. Luckily, I got a good student and somehow immediately fell comfortably into this new role. An acquaintance from the French bookstore called me to tell me that a refugee from Poland, who had escaped the German occupation in 1939, was seeking a teacher and I took him on. He was a young Pole who already spoke some French and was concerned about correct pronunciation. Fortunately, I found out accidentally after the first lesson that he was a spy. I decided to discontinue the lessons. I asked him to tell me about his flight from Poland and he happily informed me that he was involved in politics. Expressing regret, I answered that I was afraid to give him lessons, as I had no possibility to leave should the Germans arrive. He understood and we parted. I don't know what happened to him, but, on their arrival, the Germans arrested immediately the Russian from whom he had rented a room. This was a fortunate riddance, but I didn't know then how much of my future would involve teaching French.

In June 1941, Germany invaded Soviet Russia, but only after taking some preventive actions in the Balkans, concerned that Yugoslavia and Greece might side with Britain. During the tense spring of 1941 events precipitated in Yugoslavia. For over a year, Germany had been pressing it to either join the Axis, or at least to declare neutrality.

On March 25, 1941, under heavy pressure from Hitler, Yugoslav regent, Prince Paul, signed on to the Tripartite Pact with the Axis powers. Two days later a military coup under General Simovi , with tacit British support, deposed him. The plotters proclaimed the adolescent Peter II king of Yugoslavia. That did it. The Germans interpreted this coup as allying Yugoslavia implicitly with Britain and declared war on April 6,

1941, a day that changed my mother's life and mine. Meanwhile, the United States still slept while Japan marched in China and into French Indochina.

March 31, 1941. I have decided to take my son away from Belgrade. From an acquaintance in the German embassy I gathered that the city will be subject to the severest bombing.

Meanwhile, Father, age seventy-nine, lies today in a Russian hospital in Panchevo, in the Banat, across the Danube, not far from Belgrade. I took money and clothing to him in the morning. At 10:00 p.m. my son and I boarded a train to Zagreb. I had bought tickets beforehand and a friend helped us struggle through the already restive crowds in the railroad station.

My mother decided on Zagreb, in Croatia, because she had friends there and because the Croatian nationalists were known to favor Germany, hence making a bombing of Zagreb unlikely. I remember that night well, the Belgrade railroad station filled with anarchic crowds gripped by prewar panic. For me, the ensuing train ride was a defining event, as such days must have been for many boys my age throughout Europe. I was turning ten and stood in the corridor of the tense and overcrowded train thinking, "This is it. From now on I am a man. Life begins."

The Second War - Entering the Whirlpool

O n April, 1, 1941, my mother and I arrived in Zagreb. Five days later the Germans invaded Yugoslavia and, as predicted, bombed Belgrade heavily. Her diary speaks:

April 3, 1941. In Zagreb, thinking of Father. Today, in threatened Serbia, a surgeon friend must operate on him — successfully, as it turned out.

April 7, 1941. News of Belgrade's bombing on the radio. I think about Father in the hospital in Panchevo with foreboding, but fortunately the Banat was not bombed.

I am happy to have taken my son to Croatia before the start of the bombings. Zagreb wasn't bombed (validating my mother's keen instincts for survival), because Hitler promised that it wouldn't if German troops could enter without resistance. I witnessed the Germans' entry into Zagreb. Their tanks crept along, drowning in flowers. The elated crowds showered them with bouquets and the German soldiers accepted them with radiant smiles. It brought to mind "the battle of flowers" at the yearly spring festival in Nice.

My own recollections of the German arrival in Zagreb were sterner: German sergeants bellowing orders at their soldiers in amazing explosions of brutality.

Shortly, a couple appeared in Zagreb, having fled Belgrade in a panic. The husband arrived in his bedclothes and seemingly without luggage. They escaped Belgrade, fleeing Serbia precipitously for home in Croatia, across the Sava River bridge.

The arrival of the Germans laid bare latent hatreds in Yugoslavia, until then dominated by Serbs to the exasperated frustration of Croats. In the first few weeks, thousands of Serb bodies came floating down the Sava River from Croatia with their throats cut. Croats in Serbia would naturally expect retributions, though they didn't know that this would come only in the 1990s. During the war, Croats killed upward of five hundred thousand Serbs and expelled two hundred fifty thousand. They also murdered thousands of Jews and Gypsies.

April 18, 1941. I decided to return home to Belgrade. Yugoslavia had capitulated. Is Father alive? Has our apartment survived? I left my son in Zagreb for safekeeping with a trusted friend.

April 20, 1941. It is Easter and an unforgettable return to Belgrade. On the way, I slept on a hard bench leaning against the wall of the railroad car. Next to me a Yugoslav soldier lay down and fell immediately asleep, not having slept for ten nights. I had left my belongings with friends in Croatia and a kind Croatian fellow traveler carried my suitcase with food supplies. He was hurrying to retrieve his belongings in Belgrade and return as soon as possible to Croatia. I don't remember where exactly the train stopped. Fog over the Sava and a waning moon.

We crossed the river on a ferry, because the bridges had been blown up, and landed far from the city's center. First shock: proclamations in German ordering Jews to present themselves for registration, "Those who do not present themselves will be shot." Terrifying further impressions. I stop at a street faucet and drink water, forgetting about the threat of typhus, and begin walking. At first, I see no destruction, though in Zagreb they said that the city was in ruins. But now I begin to see demolished houses and the smell of burning and bodies here and there. The city looks emptied, but glass, bricks and most bodies had been removed from the streets by a few Yugoslav war prisoners. I approach our street, adjacent to the royal palace. On its corner, I am scared to see the cupola of the royal palace leaning crazily. I come closer to our house with a sinking heart. My legs shake. But the house is undamaged! I go up to the second floor with my suitcase, unlock the door and fall on my knees in the anteroom, containing my sobs. Everything is well, except for one broken window! And Father is alive and well, having survived successfully the operation and the arrival of the Germans.

May 12, 1941. Unexpectedly, my son appeared. Tanned, vigorous, well rested in the Croatian countryside, where he had stayed with an acquaintance of my friend. (My mother's friend had placed me on a train from Zagreb to Belgrade, probably with an adult acquaintance of hers.) Apparently nothing surprises him anymore, as he mentions it all in passing. He reacted little to the destruction. The city had been tidied up considerably since I first saw it three weeks earlier. Most bomb craters had been filled in, water and power functioned, and I had cleaned up the apartment.

Though my mother may not have noticed it, I was impressed by multistory houses sheared in half by bombs, with furniture in fifth or sixth floors sitting unscathed at the edge of the abyss. More memorable yet was the stench of decomposing bodies. My mother goes on to describe the life and times during the German occupation of Belgrade in 1941:

A melancholy sight on the opera square lawn: a fresh tomb under a simple, quickly hammered-together cross. Gradually, Belgrade begins to acquire a more normal aspect. Decades later, in Argentina, I read the memoirs of Goebels' secretary in which he related that upon occupying Belgrade, the commanding German general had a heart attack at the sight of the destruction.

Some Russians were among those who had suffered in Belgrade. The fate of Professor Laskarev's highly cultured family was especially tragic. In his small apartment he lived with his invalid sister, long tied to a bed, and her two single daughters. When the bombings started in the early morning of April 6, suddenly and without any warning to the civilian population, one of the daughters hurried to the attic to fetch a stretcher to take her mother to the basement. But a shrapnel tore through the roof, hit her in the temple and killed her instantly. The bombings lasted for five days, which the professor with his sister and daughters, one of them dead, spent in the basement.

Another family, consisting apparently of women and children, decided that in case of bombings they would all run to the nearby cemetery. Their nineteen-year-old mentally troubled daughter began to run frightened in another direction. She never returned. It has remained unknown where she died.

Grigori Gagarin, a young Russian geologist, was drafted in the Yugoslav army and taken prisoner. After the Yugoslav capitulation, he and other war prisoners were made to clean the streets of Belgrade by the Germans. His Serbian wife knew nothing about him during the bombings and, fetching her year-old child, fled over the Sava into Zemun to her mother on the Croatian side, crossing just before the retreating Yugoslav troops blew up the bridge. The Serbs, predominantly Anglophiles, joked that the English would rebuild that bridge for them in pure gold. Grigori was destined to perish in the Argentine Andes in the 1950s, when the car in which he traveled with fellow scientists fell over a precipice.

I knew that year-old child, his daughter, two decades later in Argentina. By then she was a very pretty young woman.

And more about Belgrade. During a bombing, a Russian and his fifteen-year-old daughter took refuge in their cellar. He was killed, while holding her in a strong embrace. The girl was wounded and the bombing continued. When neighbors rushed in to help the wounded girl, they found that her father wouldn't let her go — his corpse had stiffened in the meantime.

Those who experienced the German bombings of Belgrade told me that only the Russian church, where General Wrangel (great White Army hero) was buried, continued to function. And only the

Russian clinic operated, providing emergency medical help despite the bombings.

Water and power were restored fairly quickly in Belgrade after the Germans entered, but with power the Germans performed a crafty maneuver. In October 1941, they declared that the August electricity bill (the year's lowest) would establish the base for every family. Our share amounted to only 4 kilowatts in twenty-four hours. We installed a "Swedish" box. In it we placed a pot of soup into a box of crumpled newspapers immediately upon it having come to a boil. The box continued the cooking and within a couple of hours the soup was ready to eat.

Soon the Germans hanged five men on Terazie, the city's main square. An acquaintance who lived on that square told me that one of the unfortunates shouted "I am not guilty!" The next day, I took my son for a walk, as usual. We had to pass very close to the square, but I succeeded in distracting him with conversation and to turn his head in the opposite direction as we passed the dreadful sight.

In the middle of that summer, they found unexpectedly the corpse of E.E. Kovalevski (a friend of my mother). He had perished during the German bombings in April 1941, far from his home. They recognized him by his beard.

In 1940, my mother had hired a tutor for me Johnny, a young American of Russian extraction. His parents had immigrated to the coal mines of Pennsylvania, but he wanted to become an Orthodox priest and came to Yugoslavia to train in a Serbian seminary. We hiked together a good deal. One summer day, in 1941, we saw an important German general speeding into Belgrade at the head of an impressive motorcade. I wonder now what Johnny thought. At that time, Germany and the United States were not yet at war and he was the citizen of a neutral country. But destiny caught up with him. After the United States entered the war, he went underground, joined a guerilla group, and was caught and shot by the Germans. One war destiny among millions.

Toward winter, Father was lucky to secure a ton of coal through acquaintances. That way we could afford to heat his office, where he also slept. That winter was cold: down to minus 29 degrees centigrade (-20 ° Fahrenheit). Washing oneself was painful, as was generally living under these conditions.

I well remember that winter and the following, studying in my room in freezing temperatures, bundled in several layers of clothing. Painful indeed. Few photos now in my mother's album. Mostly of me, with my class in school; with my grandfather looking sad, in front of a Christmas tree. Few of my mother. Some photos she cut out of newspapers, showing the destruction of Belgrade from German and from American bombings.

Yugoslavia had surrendered, but many of its people didn't. First hundreds, then thousands retreated into the mountains and began a guerrilla war against the Germans that lasted four years until Germany's final defeat. At one point, the Germans needed to deploy several divisions in Yugoslavia that they critically needed elsewhere.

Periodic assassinations of German soldiers and officers took place during those occupation years. The Germans reacted drastically. Within days of their arrival, they posted notices throughout Belgrade announcing that for every German soldier killed, they would shoot one hundred Serbian civilian hostages. And they did. In 1942 it became known that a German officer had been shot in the provincial Serbian city of Kragujevac. The killer appeared to be a secondary school student. The Germans marched all four hundred boys and their teachers into the school yard and shot them all. Just one such episode. Hatred grew. My mother continues under a heading "1941-1944:"

Gray, monotonous years stretched on. In 1918, when the Germans occupied Kiev, not having yet invented the Gestapo, they behaved outwardly decently, not causing harm to the local population. Now, in Belgrade, the Germans generally didn't bother Russians, but, of course, persecuted Jews. I only once got to see a group on a street with stars of David sown to their backs being convoyed by two Germans. All these people, ladies and men, were very well dressed and went silently with harried, distressed expressions. But where were their children and what did these parents feel?

Among Russians there were only twenty Jews. Years later, in the United States, I found out why they hadn't been arrested. Among

Russian émigrés there was a man who had somehow met a friendly German before the war. When Belgrade fell to the Germans, that "friendly German" turned up in a very influential position. The courageous Russian went to see him to ask that the Jews not be touched. The German promised to take care of it immediately and told him that the Jews should not worry. He added that if he were transferred, that he would take care of them by speaking about it with his replacement. I concluded that even among Nazis there was an underground.

With the advent of winter, Gypsy children appeared on the streets. They sat on the snow and stretched out their hands, attempting to evoke pity in passersby.

Meanwhile and immediately upon the Germans' arrival in spring 1941, the Gestapo created a concentration camp on the outskirts of Belgrade in which they murdered over the following four years twenty-three thousand Jews, Gypsies and communists. None of which the population at large knew until after the war. We had no direct awareness of the Gestapo and saw only the regular German army in the streets. Those Germans behaved distantly, but correctly.

We all listened to the radio covering our heads with blankets. (The Germans forbade listening to the BBC and other allied radio stations under the penalty of death.) It was interesting how truth got distorted. The English and the Germans explained differently the death of Bulgarian Tsar Boris — and so it went for every important event. Otherwise, the radio played German music, mainly operettas, neglecting Mozart or Beethoven. The song "Lily Marlene" enjoyed extraordinary success. It played at 10:00 p.m. every night, sung by an enticing female voice, with such tender and passionate longing that even allied soldiers listened to it, as I found out after the war. Not only in Europe, but even in North Africa, British soldiers tuned in to Belgrade at 10:00 p.m.

But more about life under the German occupation. Many rumors circulated and fortune tellers, it was said, became richer by the day. People who worked for the Germans lived well, as did those who engaged in the black market. For everyone else, the days passed full of deprivations, difficulties and variations of unpleasantness. The stores had emptied, looted even before the arrival of the Germans. It seems that this was the case throughout Europe. When a city was bombed, its streets stood empty. During the following five or six hours, before the occupiers entered, people who had awaited that moment emerged from cellars and basements and started to loot. First, they broke into food stores, then shoe and clothing stores, and so forth. They only didn't touch flower shops and bookstores.

Life began to mend somehow. What joy at the first streetcars running and telephones working! Peasants brought milk, butter, meat and other produce, taking great risks in defying German authorities. (The peasants hid all their products from the Germans, who would otherwise confiscate them for their troops.) City people bought everything. Some friends were offered a "lamb," though with its feet cut off. Our friends figured out that it was a dog, but bought and ate it anyway. Our meat ration was 250 grams (9 ounces) a month and we ate horseflesh more than once. During that first Christmas of German occupation only Christmas trees and lemons appeared on the market.

But the war continued and as the peasants became smarter, they stopped accepting paper money. Thus some acquaintances exchanged their new dining room furniture for an 80 kg bag of potatoes (176 pounds). They had children, a condition that precluded being choosy.

The German invasion of the Soviet Union, in June 1941, presented White Russian émigrés with a dilemma. Germany was now at war with their mortal enemy, communism. Thus, Germany seemed a natural ally in a common struggle and many émigrés wanted to join in the battle against communism. They didn't want to fight under the German flag, however, but under their own. This, the Germans wouldn't even consider. Also the Nazis portrayed Russians as an inferior race, in any case. In fact, the Nazis devoted a propaganda periodical, entitled *Untermensch* (*Subhuman*), solely to proving that Russians were no better than animals. On the Eastern front, they treated Russians with total inhumanity. White Russians simply could not fight under a German flag and justified at times German suspicions. After the war, my mother found out that my father's niece and my cousin, Marina Alferova and her husband were shot by the Gestapo in Berlin, in 1944, for Russian nationalistic activities.

The Russian émigré community in Belgrade was now headed by (former White Russian) General Kreiter. Among outstanding émigrés was Colonel Skorodumov, who wanted to create a Russian unit to fight the Reds on the Eastern front. Germans, of course, refused him because he wanted to fight under a Russian flag.

The window of our dining room opened on a small courtyard belonging to the former Yugoslav Interior Ministry. That building was now occupied by the Gestapo. On a Sunday, in May or June 1941, my son and I spent a day in the countryside. On returning in the evening, I was surprised to see Skorodumov, whom I knew by sight, sitting in a Gestapo office opposite our window. I began to observe prudently. Now Skorodumov sat smiling pleasantly, as a German civilian spoke to him. It was evident that the conversation did not go well. Our colonel answered monosyllabically and seemed to think intensely about something. His face did not express fear. Soon another man replaced the bald-headed German, after which they brought dinner with Wienerschnitzels on a tray. The arrested colonel didn't touch it. He seemed to answer distractedly to the questions he was being asked. I thought that Skorodumov behaved very well.

Among our compatriots, some of the more foresightful gradually and quietly, moved to Germany, some to Italy. But this required many troublesome formalities. People with German surnames, principally from Croatia and Slovenia, enjoyed a special position during the German occupation. They all spoke German and the Germans called them Volksdeutsche (ethnically German) and favored them. But it turned out that not all of them lived well. Once, in my son's German school, a Volksdeutscher fellow pupil approached him during recess and asked, "Show me what you have for a snack." (It was bad cheese, on bad bread.) My son immediately handed him his sandwich, "Please take it." During these difficult years, despite trying circumstances, my son was able to keep his moral values to serve him in his later life. (As I translate this, I blush.)

On a late afternoon, in early 1943, as I was leaving my German school, I walked by a group of Volksdeutsche boys huddling in the school yard. Normally, I had friendly relations with them, but as I approached they fell silent and turned away from me. The next day I found out that they had just learned that the Germans had lost the battle of Stalingrad. This catastrophic news must have shocked them out of any illusions, because until then German propaganda had described nothing by victories in Soviet Russia. Now their tide had turned.

Things didn't turn out well for many Volksdeutsche. Though some left for Germany early on in the war, others stayed till the end of the German occupation. When in September 1944 I traveled from Belgrade to Vienna in a cattle wagon, fleeing the oncoming Soviets, there were Volksdeutsche on the train sharing our circumstances. They seemed nervous and depressed, having abandoned all their possessions which they had built up over several generations in Serbia.

In early 1943 a journalist from Berlin visited us. He wore a German uniform. Russian friends had directed him to us. He had spent six months in German-occupied Kiev and told us much that was interesting. He considered it more than probable that Hitler had already lost the war and he thought that many Germans thought so too. He praised the Russian population, which he thought had preserved its dignity despite the many privations. When he was returning to Germany in late fall of 1942, he saw Russian women walking, carrying bundles on their backs and leaning on sticks. There were so many of them, that the Germans stopped their car and asked, "Where are you going?" All gave the same answer, "I am going to look for my husband. He is a war prisoner."

My mother was very moved by this affirmation of the Russian woman's spirit of devotion, akin to her own sense of duty. Her informant didn't mention, or didn't know, that in the meantime the Germans were systematically killing 3.5 million of these prisoners through shootings, starvation, and slave labor. Almost two million Soviet soldiers had surrendered to the Germans in the first two months of the war, many thinking that they were being liberated from communism. Only after they understood the true nature of the German invasion did Russian soldiers stop surrendering and began to fight, saving Stalin's hide.

In 1942, trains from German-occupied areas of Russia came through Belgrade, carrying Russian civilians fleeing the war-torn Soviet Union, endeavoring somehow to reach the West. They knew that as the Germans left, communism would return and anything was better than that. I went several times with my son to the Belgrade railroad station, where we spoke with some of these people who lived on straw in cattle wagons. We learned firsthand what we already knew secondhand about the horrors of Stalinist murders and the utter terror under which the population lived. This only strengthened my determination never to find myself under communism again.

Formally, the Germans maintained no relationships with the Serbian population, but behaved outwardly correctly; as for the Gestapo, we knew nothing then. Once my son and I saw a small crowd surrounding a young German officer. He stood crestfallen. In front of him sprawled on the sidewalk his Doberman pincher, evidently badly wounded, possibly run over by a car. People observed with curiosity to see what the German would do — he had lost a friend, a combat comrade. The dog looked imploringly at his master. The officer slowly took out his pistol. I took my son away quickly. A shot rang.

The naiveté of the German authorities was amazing. Since they forbade photographing military objectives, I collected photos from the newspapers. Those very military objectives appeared constantly in the Serbian newspapers. For instance, under the headline "Spring trimming of trees," a photo showed the Gestapo building behind the trees. Or, "Swimmer doesn't fear cold water in winter," shown against the backdrop of a bridge previously blown up. As the Germans allowed sending newspapers abroad, Serbs kept sending them to neutral Turkey for the information of the Allies (while those very Allies kept bombing them almost daily).

The movies are showing a historic film — the freeing of Mussolini from prison in the Apennines. I don't remember whether Skorzeny landed in a helicopter or a plane, but he landed in the tiniest space. The Duce, in a black overcoat and black helmet, with a stony expression hurried to board the plane.

This was, in 1943, a sensational event. Fascist Italy had surrendered. The Allies had captured Mussolini and kept him on top of the Gran Sasso, Italy's tallest mountain south of the Alps. Skorzeny was an SS officer who landed a small plane in an incredibly exiguous space to the amazement of the Allied soldiers guarding Mussolini. Skorzeny and his men overwhelmed them. The Germans, already reeling, were very proud of this feat. Of course, we had no news from the Allied side.

By that time too, the war's strategic situation had evolved. Though outwardly Germany still held together, it had no possibility of winning the war, despite brave propaganda. In retreat in Russia, with the Allies having landed in Italy and progressing slowly north, the Germans awaited Eisenhower's invasion, not knowing when and where it would come.

November 30, 1943. Sirens are howling. Several times our radio was taken off the air, but so far, thank God, the Americans have not bombed us. I am trying not to think frightening thoughts, but my soul goes dead when the radio falls silent. Does my son worry? A new existence has taken over: we prepare warm clothing and other essentials every evening. My son lays out his clothes and overcoat before going to bed, after which he falls asleep undisturbed. Father remains imperturbable and I admire his self-control. They have bombed Skoplje (in present-day Macedonia) and Nish (in southern Serbia). We live under Damocles' sword.

January 6, 1944 (Russian Christmas Eve). Night alarm at 2:00 a.m., but after the allclear we sat under the Christmas tree that we had already decorated.

January 31, 1944. Yesterday my son and I fasted (in religious observance). As he went to bed, he declared that he wanted to confess (in church) and I supported that of course.

A few days ago, the lights went out at 9:15 p.m. Father had already gone to bed, but hadn't yet fallen asleep and I decided not to wake up the boy. I was dressed and everything was ready, as usual. I prayed, "Lord, let this pass us by also this time."

Today (no date indicated), I became tired painting windows dark blue and otherwise making them invisible from the outside, following orders published in the newspaper. Doing this is nauseating if one thinks about the reason. My son, thankfully, helps. (The Germans ordered that all windows be blackened in some fashion, so that American bombers couldn't see any lights in Belgrade during night bombings.) Despite it all, we continue to live as though nothing abnormal were happening: everyday housekeeping concerns, meetings with friends.

April 3, 1944. I have just interrupted a French lesson. The siren began howling and my student let me go right away. Fortunately, there was no bombing.

April 9, 1944. Last night, on the eve of Catholic Easter, there were two alarms with expeditions to the cellar. This time they bombed us. In the morning my son found bomb shrapnel in the yard of our apartment building. It reminded me how I used to find such fragments in our Kiev garden during the civil war.

April 16, 1944. It began at 9:00 a.m. and lasted until noon. Terrifying and fatiguing. It is our Easter and for us our battle initiation. The actual bombing began around 11:00 a.m. We sat in the cellar, covering our heads with overcoats to protect ourselves from shrapnel. Friends living in a four-story house suffered. The building, in which many other Russians lived as well, was completely destroyed. By a miracle, no one died. Our neighborhood didn't suffer damage, but a kilometer away there was much destruction. Many have loaded their belongings on carts and started walking to the outskirts of the city.

April 17, 1944. Several alerts "in vain," a quiet night. But around noon today, a second bombing attack. It seemed stronger than the first and the damage came closer to our neighborhood. A nauseating moment when one hears on the radio that "they are nearing." There was a moment when it rocked us. It means that a bomb fell close. My whole being prays, "Lord make it pass by us." I don't even have strength for a longer prayer. We are all tired and that perhaps adds to the fear. They give us electric power, water, and telephone intermittently.

April 18, 1944. I stepped out of the house today for errands in the neighborhood. The streets have emptied. Fortunately, the weather has turned warmer. Fresh ruins and everywhere broken glass underfoot. New alert. I am running home.

April 21, 1944. After three quiet days, a small bombing. The city and our apartment house have emptied. Some, having exhausted strength and food supplies, return home in the evenings to sleep overnight. The telephone has begun to work. My son has roseola and I have a cold and some fever.

April 28, 1944. The electric power has returned. My mother's diary doesn't record the almost daily bombings during this period, which destroyed electric power, telephone lines, and water pipes.

May 7, 1944. They bombed the bridge over the Danube, far from us and it lasted only ten minutes, not long enough to frighten us. Yesterday, Sunday, people expected another bombing for some reason and the city emptied almost completely. We have resisted leaving, not so much from courage as from impotence (small boy, old father). These days, many write their wills in an informal manner; we did too, though beside what's in the apartment, we have nothing to bequeath.

May 17, 1944. They connected the water, though only briefly. There was an alert, while the Americans bombed the Rumanian oil fields in Ploesti. I managed to get my son out of the school and home on time. We and our neighbors are now sitting in a cellar, a few houses away — it seems somewhat better than other cellars, but we don't know whether it is as good as we hope. We languished there till noon. I became tired watching for our belongings and keeping an eye on my boy, who ran home for a flashlight and tin pistol to play with suitable company.

It is now reasonably comfortable to shelter in the cellar, but what will we do in winter, if we live that long? My son will be starting the fourth grade of gymnasium (the equivalent of American eighth grade).

May 18, 1944. Though under a cloudy sky, we were bombed today nonetheless and the city has suffered.

June 6, 1944. Alerts have now become daily events. Today, they bombed the railroad station, but we have become so inured that we reacted calmly, the more so in the new cellar, where due to its isolation we can hear little of what is going on in the city. The Allies have landed in France today.

June 11, 1944. The Germans built pools throughout the city to extinguish fires caused by the bombings. There is a pool near the parliament building and I let my son go swim there, insisting that he close his mouth when swimming. When he returns, I place him immediately under a shower.

A friend has given me a big book: "Niva" for the year 1902 (an extremely popular annual magazine in prerevolutionary Russia). Toward the end of this tome, a comment refers to a famous medium, Madame de Thèbes: she prophesied that the twentieth century would be marked by bloody wars and revolutions. The magazine's editor exclaims: "Who can believe that, in our civilized century?" Meanwhile the bombs just kept on pelting us.

I remember the words of a young scientist friend who told me that he grew up on a derelict city lot. My son is playing in ruins of bombed-out buildings, on which weeds have grown. He calls that place, without irony, a meadow.

July 20, 1944. A failed attempt against the "Führer's" life produced a great impression. A friend said, "This means that not all Germans are satisfied." These were, of course, times of tightest German censorship. German propaganda conveyed an uncontested impression of total support for Hitler.

July 24, 1944. Again an alert, but without bombing. After the allclear we went immediately to church.

An old Russian with a long beard wanders around the streets. He carries a large cross and proclaims in a loud and monotone voice: "Repent! Repent!" Serbs pass him by with sympathetic smiles.

The Americans now bomb us regularly. Every morning, at 9:00 a.m., I serve Father a second cup of what is now called "coffee" (consisting of roasted chicory). Before the bombing starts, the radio reports in German: "The enemy airplanes are now over Milan, Venice, Ljubljana, Zagreb." Thereafter they usually begin dropping bombs somewhere. A Russian woman shouts from a balcony in our backyard: "Has the professor had his second cup of coffee? That means it's time to go to the cellar."

After one particularly noisy bombing, a drunken Russian neighbor shouted to my son, Alexander: "Sasha, Russian soul, don't be afraid" (not that I ever was — it all seemed so normal then). A bomb hit his school, to the delight of the lazier boys. We now continue to go to bed routinely fully dressed for the night alerts.

Lately the Germans have authorized corresponding with Germany. This allowed me to contact Austrian friends in Vienna, whom I had known since the 1920s. They promised to place at our disposal their son's room in their apartment. He had been drafted by the Germans and was taken prisoner by the Soviets (but survived and returned after the war!). In the meantime I was preparing our flight, much before the end of the war.

The Soviets were by now advancing through Rumania and the Germans retreating. Under no conditions would my mother experience the Soviets again.

Oh, beastly twentieth century! Virulent totalitarian deformations of socialism in mortal combat with each other, communists versus Nazis and fascists — and ultimately both against liberal capitalism. We sat in our cellars in Serbia, not a party to these conflicts, being bombed, killed, and deprived of all rights, human and otherwise, even to water. The same was happening to Filipinos, Burmese, Estonians, or Italians, and to so many others around the globe. Now, decades later, in lawful, peaceful California it all seems so monstrous. It seemed so natural then to a boy.

Through the Rapids

By mid-1944, the Soviets were rolling up German armies across the entire eastern front, from the Baltic to the Balkans. Of immediate concern to my mother, the Reds were now in Rumania, bringing her fate and mine to a decisive turn.

I had firmly decided to flee once the Reds would occupy Ploesti, in Rumania. Many Russians were leaving Serbia. My son and I were among the last to join in this "migration of the nations." Waves of refugees flooded into Germany. Fortunately, the Germans placed no particular obstacles, as they retreated slowly, but systematically. Very many fled, not only Russian émigrés from Poland and the Baltic countries, but also people from the entire Soviet Union.

I packed a trunk and suitcases, trying to decide beforehand what was possible and thought of sending the trunk ahead to Vienna. I had all the necessary immunizations done to my son and we both had our teeth cleaned. No fillings were needed. Before the war, my son took fish oil daily, but now it was impossible to procure (oh, joy!). To my grief, Father, who was now eighty-one, refused categorically to travel with us, even though he had undergone successfully a second, unavoidable surgery. I left him the address of our friends in Vienna, our next intended destination. We both thought that we were parting forever.

We left Belgrade on August 31, 1944. The city fell to the Red Army on October 20. PM Bermondt-Avalov, White-Russian friend of General Heinz Guderian, helped Russians leave. I remember him with gratitude.

Pavel Bermondt-Avalov arose as a classic figure of stormy revolutionary times. He styled himself a descendant of Georgian princes, began his military career as a Russian army band leader, switched to regular combat troops, fought in the Russo-Japanese war and in World War I, moving up through the ranks. After the Bolshevik coup, he joined the Whites, but then struck out on his own, now a major-general. He recruited a mostly German-speaking Baltic force to prevent Latvia and Lithuania from becoming independent countries. Defeated, he fled to Germany, where he eventually ran afoul of the Nazis, who expelled him to Yugoslavia. He retained German connections, including General Guderian, with whom he had become friends during the turbulent 1920s. I knew Bermondt-Avalov in his old age, still a rather charming, dapper adventurer. He died in New Paltz, New York, eulogized by two women.

A friend assisted us onto the train. We traveled in full refugee comfort, in a fourth-class car for horses. I put down a blanket on the straw and surrounded it with our suitcases. We lay down and were on our way. There traveled Russians in all the cars. Some comfortably — one family ate normally, as their nanny cooked. Others managed as well as they could. I forgot much, but the arrival in Budapest stayed in my memory. The siren began to wail. They uncoupled the engine, took it away, and stranded us exposed in the middle of the railroad yard. Many travelers ran away in all directions. But the railroad station was so demolished already that I decided to stay on the train. American planes strafed the station. My son and I lay under my fur coat for some twenty minutes, but all ended well.

Among Russians on the train was also another lady with a boy. From a distance I could see that a frightened expression never strayed from her face. Later, in Austria, she told me that she had learned that on our train traveled some Yugoslav men of a blue-collar worker type who concluded that we were all fleeing because we had collaborated with the Germans and that therefore it would be proper to kill us. I was lucky not to have heard about their plans earlier.

Those were incongruous times. All normal assumptions became scrambled and the most surprising turns of events now appeared but unremarkable. On the train, I struck up a conversation with a youngish, seemingly uneducated Serb. He revealed that he was a communist, possibly one of those who thought that we should be killed. Why was he traveling to Germany at that moment? Nevertheless, I liked him. He spoke, among other things, of his great admiration for Tito, "the greatest man in the world." I scoffed to my son about that, but history proved Tito to be a man much larger than his otherwise peripheral country would warrant.

It took us six days to reach Vienna (normally a twelve-hour train ride) and I thought that they were the longest days of my life. We arrived tired from the difficult conditions on the train.

At the border between Hungary and Austria-Germany, we experienced unknowingly a "concentration camp," surrounded by barbed wire and with barracks for inmates. That border, I now realize, was run by the Gestapo. They herded us, separated men from women, had us strip naked and ran us through showers, the same kind that could alternatively be converted to water or to gas. Afterwards they examined us closely one by one. They measured my cranium to make sure I wasn't Jewish. It seemed a joke to a thirteen-year old boy. Only much later did I understand the sinister implications.

September 5, 1944. We arrived in Vienna in the early morning, on a clear, sunny day. Amazing peace reigned over the city. The streetcars functioned, all stores were open and with a fair stock of merchandise — everything normal. We arrived at my friends', where a cordial reception and a room awaited us. The room belonged to my friend Olga's son. He had been conscripted by the Germans and sent to the eastern front. Now there was no news from him and tears often streamed on Olga's face. I wrote to Father right away and put the letter into a mailbox — also normal.

Olga and her husband were elderly by then. They were old Vienna in every sense and the husband had been a general in the Habsburg Empire's army in World War I.

We transported our entire luggage, which I had left at the railroad station's checkroom, by streetcar. Our first moments in Vienna didn't pass, however, without my son nearly causing me a heart attack. Upon arriving, I left him at the railroad station's restaurant, while I went out to find a transportation means to my friends' house. I enjoined him not to leave our fourteen pieces of luggage under any circumstances while I was away. I cannot describe my shock, when a few minutes later I saw him on the street looking for me — without our luggage. I rushed into the restaurant and fortunately all our things were still there.

September 9, 1944. The first bombing alert!

September 21, 1944. We have been in Vienna for sixteen days now. Though not on the first day, I felt an indescribable weariness, but I couldn't lose any time in organizing our immediate future. I had no money, but I brought for bribing purposes one thousand Serbian cigarettes and slivovitz (Serbian plum-based vodka) in small bottles. Both became greatly useful.

Thoughts about Father torment me. The radio signal from Belgrade is still in German, which means that the city hasn't fallen yet to the Soviets. What must the poor old man endure? Days pass in organizational concerns and worries about our further progress westward. It's better that way: it makes me forget about our situation — "a leaf in the wind." I have placed my son immediately into one of the better gymnasiums, the Schottenbastei.

My mother, of course, had no confidence that the Germans would hold off the Reds and consequently viewed our stay in Vienna as merely transitional. Her goal was to get me into neutral Switzerland. My Swiss godmother had obtained a Swiss entry visa for me — an almost unimaginable privilege in those days.

October 7, 1944. Battles in the suburbs of Belgrade. What does poor Father feel? He is alone at such a time. Here, the siren howls daily now and I go nowhere without my son, so that a bombing would not find us separated. Today we sat in a bomb shelter for three hours. My son appears unfazed. He always carries a book and I some knitting. We are getting used to it.

October 11, 1944. A letter from Father, dated September 28, and immediately thereafter another, dated October 5. He sent us his blessings, "Don't worry about me, I have everything." (?) I cried. Belgrade radio is silent today. Vienna was bombed by Americans twice these days, but far from us.

October 20, 1944. Unexpected letter from Father dated October 11: concerned about us and asks us not worry about him.

October 22, 1944. In the news, battles in the southern suburbs of Belgrade. Four years later, when I was finally able to extract Father from then communist Yugoslavia, he told me that the Germans defended each house in their retreat. There was a moment when in front of our house stood artillery and an officer was shouting "zurück!" "zurück" ("back!" "back") so loudly that Father could hear even in our apartment which was in the rear of the building, despite all the noise and his elderly hearing.

I await information from the gymnasium. My son has not yet been officially admitted. I keep him constantly near me, so that we endure the alerts together.

Well, not exactly. In those initial weeks in Vienna, when life was still fairly normal, I spent much of each day on streetcars helping the conductor with switches, which allowed me to explore the entire city and its surroundings for free. A wonderful memory of personal independence. My mother did not object.

More news. Officially, Belgrade fell yesterday or on the twentieth. Unexpectedly, a letter from Father, dated September 11, trying to console me!

Undated. While we sat in the cellar, the light kept blinking, a sign of bombs falling, and it kept blinking without interruption for some ten minutes. But an explosion shook us only once. After the allclear, we saw ruins all around, ambulances racing and worn-out faces among the rare passersby. Around the corner from our building stood the Augustinerkirche. It survived. In 1920, we had listened in it to Richard Strauss conducting his own compositions, but the wheels of history keep turning.

Undated. During alerts we kept meeting two older ladies in a shelter, apparently sisters. A great sorrow had apparently befallen them — they were grieving over someone. Soon authorities published an order not to take pets into the bomb shelters and at our next encounter they came without their little dog. Next day they told us that they found their little friend dead under the bed. During one bombing, a Russian acquaintance opened her purse when the bombs started falling. She had in it an icon of the Mother of God and she began to pray silently. During an explosion, an Austrian woman moved next to her, looked into the purse, and asked, "May I also?" Our acquaintance said, "But of course, please."

I have sown a few of Mother's jewels in my belt and Alexander carries a backpack with documents.

Infinite formalities absorb me in my hopes to enter Switzerland, where we had some money. We were invited to Switzerland by an old Swiss friend from my Kiev adolescence, officially my son's godmother. To travel across Austria, now Germany, was very difficult. As the Germans retreated and the front neared, our Russian compatriots strained all resources to betake themselves father west. It was difficult to obtain a German travel permit. I know of people who walked from Vienna to Salzburg (156 miles)!

I cannot imagine by what means we could have left Vienna if fate had not taken pity on us. (Well, it wasn't fate: it was my mother's initiative and energy.) Every week I went to the Swiss General Consulate to find out whether we had received a visa. It seemed that the consul had time on his hands and he received me personally. We talked, about politics mostly. I needed to work in order to qualify for food coupons for my son and for myself. On one occasion, he advised me to speak with the Swedish consul general. He added, "I doubt that he can place you to work with a Swedish family, but the present consul has a Russian wife. Perhaps she could help you."

I was very reluctant to appear in the role of supplicant, troubling unknown people. It was now around October 19 or 20, Belgrade had fallen to the Reds, and my soul was disconsolate. This was no time to be squeamish. After three weeks, I called and gave my last name. The consul's Russian wife came to the phone immediately. In an extraordinary twist of destiny, she told me that she was related to the Kugushevs from Odessa and hence a distant part of our family. She gave me right away an appointment for the next day. Upon acquaintance, I found her to be a typical St. Petersburg lady (a highly positive evaluation in my mother's view). She was in her early fifties.

After a brief conversation, she left and returned with her husband, Einar Ytterberg, a formal, dapper, erect, graying, rosy-cheeked, unsmiling diplomat. He exuded passionate hatred for Hitler and tender love for the French. In fact, on further acquaintance, he proved a fanatical admirer of Napoleon. We spoke a little in French and then he said, "I cannot offer you a salary, but if every evening between 7:00 and 10:00 p.m. you would listen to phone calls from our embassies in Budapest and Berlin, you and your son will receive diplomatic food coupons (milk, butter, bread, etc.) and the right to use the diplomatic anti-bombing bunker." His offer stunned me, as I felt particularly vulnerable and uncertain about the future. I called in my son, who was waiting on the street, and he apparently produced a good impression, because he spoke French fluently. The next day I began to "work." My obligations included an inspection of the entire building before going to bed. I had to feel all windows with my hands in absolute darkness, as all windows were darkened in case of a night alert.

They expected Budapest to fall to the Soviets imminently, though it didn't until February 1945.

As the Soviets advanced through the Balkans and the Germans retreated, the twentieth century's hate-fueled ideologies reached some climactic showdowns. During Nazi Germany's waning last stand, the most extreme and violent fascists came to power in Rumania and in Hungary — the Iron Guard in Rumania and the Arrow-Cross in Hungary. Arrow-Cross thugs continued to export Jews to German concentration camps to the last minute. We saw them, racing wild-eyed through Vienna in increasingly tense days preceding the arrival of the Soviets. Communists, badly mauled during the Nazi era in Rumania, Hungary, and Slovakia, now arrived on the coattails of the Soviets. As the Red Army entered, house-to-house battles and unspeakable cruelties followed. Communism now dominant, triumphed for two more generations.

The consulate functioned in the building of the former Swedish embassy in Austria. It ceased to be an embassy after Germany absorbed Austria in 1938, but it continued to be called "the Swedish Palais." Its rooms and halls were now almost empty. All valuable items had been transferred to a countryside castle, with the exception of some mirrors and marble busts. The building reminded me somewhat of our house in Kiev, built by architect Baron Stein for himself at the end of the nineteenth century. Our house had fewer rooms and halls, but we had marble balconies and fireplaces and better ceilings.

My adolescent memory of this palace was quite different. I remember it full of Napoleonic mementos and *premier empire* furniture. Einar Ytterberg cherished a passionately idealized vision of the Napoleonic France — all romance of war and glory. The building's atmosphere left an enduring impression on me, especially as I was reading *War and Peace* at that time, with its stories of Russia's war with Napoleon.

November 5, 1944. The strongest bombing yet! Fortunately, while it was going on, my son was reading his current Karl May (an extremely popular German author of adventure books for boys) and I was knitting my green "alert" sweater, on which I worked in bomb shelters. A bomb fell some twenty meters from us and hit the house next to ours. When we emerged from the cellar, we saw a gaping ruin next door and all around a layer of dust. Upstairs in our house there was also dust and broken windows. Fortunately I had remembered to open our windows and the glass held. The building's entrance door was torn off its hinges. Our poor general is cleaning away the debris. I can imagine how he suffers as an Austrian patriot and officer witnessing what is going on.

November 19. Father's eighty-second birthday. Is he alive? We have been bombed again.

Finally, I found another school for my son. Bombings have destroyed my son's original gymnasium, to his gleeful satisfaction. In the new school, they accepted him with the proviso that he would pass a third-grade gymnasium exam by Easter. I react little to this disappointment, because in our times Easter is very far away.

November 28. I don't know how much longer it remains for us to live. In daytime we began to use the new, diplomatic bunker shelters, my son with his Karl May books and I with the green sweater. I spent the evenings in the consulate's office. The American bombings have intensified and increased in frequency, but only during daytime for now. They concentrated on Vienna's inner city and burned and demolished St. Stephen's cathedral and the Opera House among other landmarks dear to Viennese hearts. So far they didn't touch our neighborhood; electricity functioned and hot water flowed from the faucets.

Once we found ourselves in the shallow shelter built in the garden of the former embassy. It was at best suited for shrapnel. We all sat silently, praying probably; only occasional suppressed groans. A bomb flew by with a distinct, chilling whistle, probably not far from us. Mrs. Ytterberg exclaimed, with irritation, not fear, "How unpleasant." It was the day when a bomb fell into the Viennese Opera House.

It is possible to get somehow used to the bombings, but after the hit on the Opera House I became afraid and went to a pharmacy. I asked for something to calm the nerves. The pharmacist gave me a medication to be taken after "severe illnesses and strokes of destiny." Strokes of destiny? Exactly what we needed.

When the bombings increased, the Ytterbergs moved to the country castle and invited us to join them. By then we already lived in the consulate building, in one of the guest rooms. I was touched by their concern for us.

Once, while the Ytterbergs were away at the country castle, I received a phone call from the Swedish embassy in Budapest, informing me that the widow of the Swedish consul was traveling to Vienna and that it was necessary to help her at the railroad station in Vienna. After a hasty conference with our vice-consul and the kind old German cook, we developed a plan of action. In the evening

*arrived a distressed lady and with her a Swedish companion, who
was a Jew. An improbable encounter then, as Jews were either in
hiding, or in concentration camps. But this gentleman was a citizen
of a neutral nation. They stayed overnight. I hosted them and had
dinner served in the enormous, oak paneled dining room. I don't
remember what was served, but I believe that salami appeared on the
menu. The lady soon went to bed, but I remained to converse with
her companion, an engineer. After he learned my story and about
my decision to flee again he said, "I want to tell you something,
but give me your word that you will not tell anyone." I acquiesced,
of course. He told me that there was in Innsbruck a center of an
organization that smuggled escaped war prisoners, as well as Jews,
over mountain trails into neutral Switzerland. "Would you like us
to help you get into Switzerland?" "Thank you, no," I said "I am
afraid to expose my son to danger." I thought: how interesting! (As
for me, how I would have loved some adventure then!)*

*Soon after this, the Ytterbergs spent a couple of days in Vienna
and invited me to have dinner with them. Next to me sat a count
Meifor, an important leading Jesuit. He too showed interest in my
adventure and promised to give me a letter to all Jesuits in Europe,
asking them to provide my son and me with all possible support.
Ytterberg, though irritated by my decision to escape Vienna, also
gave me a certificate in four languages, stating that we were under
the protection of the Swedish king.*

*Earlier, an elderly Austrian, who had been a war prisoner in
Russia during World War I, expressed great surprise to hear that I
ran from my own people, "Russians are so compassionate." Later,
I am sure, he understood why I hurried to leave.*

Admirably, my mother created unique conditions for the two of us
in these storms of war. Our trajectory proved incomparably privileged
when compared to millions of other fates, battered and destroyed under
similar circumstances. Only now, decades later, have I come to appreciate
the full scope of my mother's courage, skills, and determination in
directing our destiny amid all the hazards through which we navigated.

Now I also find it remarkable how much underground functioned
under the very noses of the seemingly omnipotent Gestapo: secret

organizations smuggling people into Switzerland, Jesuit networks operating in the shadows, and who knows how many other clandestine linkages that saved doomed lives. The 1947 black and white movie *The Third Man*, set in Vienna immediately after the end of World War II, by then occupied by the four powers, captures accurately the poignant atmosphere during these final months before the arrival of the Soviets. In it, a scene takes place in a Viennese cemetery on a cold, dark winter afternoon. In late fall 1944, we had accompanied the hearse of a Russian acquaintance in that very cemetery under a similar dark and rainy sky, in the same atmosphere of foreboding uncertainty.

During my mother's nightly inspections of the consulate's building, she would glimpse indistinct figures lurking about the consulate in the darkness. Shades of *The Third Man*. What intrigues, what dramas motivated these furtive movements seeking to penetrate a neutral diplomatic building?

One day, a dapper Greek gentleman, a figure from Hollywood's central casting for a movie like *Casablanca*, appeared at the consulate with a mysterious agenda. He was in his midthirties. Men of his age were generally either fighting or serving as prisoners of one kind or another, but around him floated an aura of adventure. It remained uncertain what exactly he intended, but it was clear that he was open to any possibility and that his game included numerous exits.

The consul's driver, a weaselly Austrian in his forties, with a permanent, ambiguously friendly grin, was a Gestapo agent. He kept an eye on all of us and tried to introduce me, innocent that I was, to pornographic pictures. Even then he struck me as an unprincipled opportunist — with the Nazis today, with someone else tomorrow. A typical figure from those fluid times.

During the last weeks in Vienna we lived in almost daily mortal danger. I decided to travel under conditions I could not yet imagine. We received a German travel permit valid for three destinations: to Feldkirch, on Austria's Lichtenstein/Switzerland border, and to two other locations I now don't remember. These choices reminded me of an illustration by Bilibin of a famous Russian children's tale. An armed knight on horseback reaches a fork in the road, with a rock indicating three directions: "If you go straight, you and your horse will find death." "If left, your horse will perish.," "If right, you will die." I chose Feldkirch, but how to get there?

On the eve of our departure I packed our last suitcases. The photo albums, our most precious possessions, were already in the trunk. In it, I had brought some silverware. I shared it with Mrs. Ytterberg to somehow thank her for her cordial support; she had asked me to call her for help in packing. We left the trunk in the consulate hoping for diplomatic protection. The trunk and its contents survived. (This trunk began its career some eighty years earlier in Europe, but rests now in my possession, in Menlo Park, California.)

Frau Maas, the kindly cook, and Olga, the Estonian secretary, who was also a refugee from somewhere, came to lend me their sympathy. (I remember Olga, a woman still in her thirties, as a remarkable speaker of some twelve languages. This certainly helped her obtain a valuable job in the Swedish consulate.) "My poor dear," said Frau Mass. "But you too, Frau Maas," I said in a foreboding of what was to come. I felt no hesitation: it was necessary to escape. A few months later, when I already lived in the French occupation zone, in Western Austria, I received a letter from Olga, "You did the right thing in leaving." She was writing from Vienna, which had been overrun by the Soviets. By that time we had heard of all kinds of horrors taking place there.

Near the Swedish consulate, there was a Russian church with a very good priest, Father Constantine. He celebrated a Te Deum for us and gave my son a paper icon of St. Anthony. With God's help we got underway.

Navigating the
Last Stretch

We left Vienna eight days before the first street combats began. I got under way as on a medieval journey, guarding all my safe-conducts against my breast. Thanks to our Swedish papers, we traveled in some comfort on our trek west, in a less than full car. We passed unharmed through Sankt Pölten, a railroad hub which the Americans bombed methodically every other day and which the Germans repaired immediately just as methodically. I remember the railroad station at Wels. It was demolished to such an extent that the train crept through it at a turtle's pace; all conversation ceased, and the passengers will probably remember this sight forever.

Wels was another railroad hub systematically bombed by the Americans. Over every new mound of twisted rails sticking their severed limbs into the sky, the Germans laid a fresh set of tracks. Our train crept some fifty or sixty feet above the twisted forest of steel, seemingly into the sky. A mini Eiffel Tower. Then it descended just as cautiously to earth. An indelible scene.

Shortly after Wels we saw another memorable, but incomprehensible sight: an area surrounded by tall barbed wire fences and in it men working in striped, black-and-white prisoners' clothing. It was, we found out after the war, the Mauthausen concentration camp. We didn't understand what this meant, because most civilians in Germany didn't know about the existence of concentration camps.

I have now forgotten many details from that journey. We had to spend a night in Salzburg, now a delight of Austria's eighteenth century, but then tense and war-torn in Nazi Germany's last days. We stayed in a hotel where one wall of our room had disappeared because of a nearby bomb hit and was replaced by particle board.

In Garmisch-Partenkirchen (site of the 1936 Winter Olympics) we slept on the railroad stations benches, I don't remember why. We were traveling to Munich, where incidentally the Yurievs, Father's friends and mine, lived. They had left Belgrade earlier. It was now around April 20, 1945, Berlin had already fallen to the Reds and the Germans had transferred their capital, such as it was, into the ruins of Munich.

The destruction of Munich astounded us. Walking from the station we didn't see for the first forty-five minutes a single building standing. Nothing but mounds of stones and bricks. A diminutive, steam-engine train, on very narrow tracks, improvised in these ruins, crept through what could only be assumed to have been the city's center. We walked over nonexistent former streets, looking for Kaulbacherstrasse, where the Jesuit center was located. On the way, we passed the English garden. Complete neglect, with weeds growing five feet high, but nightingales sang their heads off. To our surprise, amid the chaotic ruins stood an entirely undamaged Jesuit monastery. A servant brought us into a reception room where we immediately sank into the chairs. An old man in a cassock entered. It seems that he was the Jesuit provincial for Bavaria. On seeing my son, he dipped into his pocket and gave the boy a candy. I don't remember about what we talked and what advice he gave us, but we left with his good wishes and the hope to be able to leave Munich.

I don't remember how, but my son and I found a room in a village on the outskirts of the city. Early next morning I went to the village post office to inquire how best to get to Munich. As I was leaving, the post office employee said, "Wait" and he gave us two cups of tea. Then he reached under the counter and brought up a loaf of bread, cut a piece and said "Stick this in your purse."

As our need to leave Germany continued I had to travel frequently into the city. We spent one night in the basement of the Munich railroad station, at that point a veritable "Grand Hotel International" because of the enormous variety of refugees. There were many Russians in Munich, as well as numerous refugees from countries in Eastern Europe. Many interesting observations. A seventeen-year-old girl told us that in searching for her parents she had already traversed the front lines between the Germans and the Soviets five times. I don't remember where and how she ate. Next to us on the ground sat a couple in their early forties from one of the Baltic countries. In their flight west from the oncoming Soviets, they found themselves in Dresden during the horrendous British bombing in February 1945 when many thousands were killed and burned. They thought that their survival could only be explained by God having a design for them. At that time, no one had yet heard about the Dresden fire holocaust.

Though the Swiss denied me a visa (they feared unemployment), I intended to convey my son to Switzerland, as he had a Swiss visa. The problem was the lack of a German exit visa, denied a fourteen-year old enemy alien (my son had French citizenship). Finally, I located the German foreign ministry, now located in a building that still stood amid the surrounding ruins, though all its windows had been replaced with boards. There I finally obtained that exit visa.

My mother, battle-hardened through a lifetime struggle against officialdoms, entered deliberately an office marked "Eintritt Verboten" "entry forbidden." In a darkened room, with boarded-up windows sat a middle-aged, formally dressed, harried-looking official, in glasses and a Nazi-party pin in his lapel. My mother explained the situation to him. He said to his secretary "Stamp on the bird," referring the German eagle, onto my passport.

At this time, less than three weeks before the German surrender, everybody knew that Germany had lost. Americans and Soviets were converging toward the middle of Germany. Yet German troops still fought and the government still functioned as best it could. Order, that most cherished German standard, still prevailed. The post office delivered the mail — if it could find the house among the rubble. Checkrooms at railroad stations remained reliable in towns where the stations had not been blown to pieces.

Mr. Yuriev, our friend from Belgrade, now living in Munich, helped us greatly. He seemed to have some influence among the local Russians and thanks to his connections we received a German authorization to travel through Innsbruck to Feldkirch, on the Swiss border. Mr. Yuriev and his wife, then in their late fifties to early sixties, had prepared bicycles for the eventuality that the Reds, not the Americans would occupy Munich (the Americans did).

The Yurievs, like millions of others had no difficulty in making an ideological decision between communist totalitarianism and liberal capitalism. Many others, however, who also fled west, were either Nazi sympathizers or outright Nazis. They made no ideological choice, but only tried to save their skins. Still, for the Germans, Americans were cultural kin, despite wartime hostility, and they feared the Russians for being essential barbarians, in addition to communist cruelty and repression.

It was April 24 by now. With my son's visa secured, we left Munich traveling south on a night train. Trains didn't run during the day for fear of American bombings and this train was completely darkened. On our way through Bavaria we saw four huge, brightly lit balloons high in the sky. We didn't know what this meant. After the war, we found out that the American air force had placed them to indicate the area of the Dachau concentration camp so that it would not be bombed. At that time we didn't know about the existence of Dachau.

The train unexpectedly left us off at Krems, a small Bavarian town. I managed to rent a room for a night and decided to check practically all our luggage, several suitcases, at the Krems railroad station. Who knows what awaits us? It's best to travel as light as possible. Immediately after the war I returned there, only to find out that French general Leclerc's Moroccan troops had looted all the checked luggage. (The savage behavior of rape and plunder of these troops matched up well against that of the Soviet armies.) But I got lucky. They only took some silver teaspoons. My belongings stood in a corner of an empty shed tied together with paper strings. For that I thanked the station chief and gave him some cigarettes from my purse. It was also he who had earlier arranged to place us on the first train out of Krems during our journey out of Munich in exchange for a small bottle of slivovitz. Amazingly, my mother had managed to keep at this late stage of our travels a trove of slivovitz bottles and cigarettes through so much thick and thin.

At length our new train made it to Innsbruck. Not without difficulty I found a room for the two of us. Now I continued to seek necessary documents to bring my son to Feldkirch, part of a forbidden frontier zone, and thence into Switzerland. For that purpose I began to visit the police (this was not the Gestapo). A nice old man kept receiving me there, a typical Austrian administration official, who did not hide his antipathy for Hitler, who by then was dead in any case, though that wasn't yet known. We parted friends.

One early morning I hurried out of our hotel in the hills above Innsbruck on my daily errand to the police headquarters. As I walked down the trail toward the city, I was surprised to see an American parachute spread over an old apple tree next to the trail. The flyer had disappeared. To come close to the tree would be dangerous because under the applicable German rule, death by firing squad would threaten — for out of such a silk parachute, thirty-six shirts could be made. Quick, quick, away. (This refers to a German rule forbidding any contacts of civilians with the enemy. My mother reacted to such rules with a paranoia equal to the times.)

We experienced our last bombings in Innsbruck. But now we are off to Feldkirch, our destination on the Lichtenstein/Swiss border. There was chaos on the trains, as people fled from fear of bombings. All train doors were completely blocked by a human mass and the only way to get into a car was through the already broken windows. Someone's arms lifted first my boy, then me into the car. In my hand I held a precious cigarette pack and dropped it on the platform. Some kind soul picked it up handed it to me.

By now it was April 26, my mother's unnoticed forty-fifth birthday. Conditions on that train were much different from the primitive, but orderly leaving from Belgrade in a cattle wagon on straw, or from our reasonably comfortable Vienna departure with our Swedish papers. On each successive leg, the train experience reflected the Götterdämmerung atmosphere of Nazidom's dissolving. Now thousands fled for their lives across Germany and hundreds of thousands, perhaps millions, from adjacent Eastern regions. Many Russians had escaped west from Soviet territories when the Germans arrived.

After the war I met in Innsbruck a Russian Orthodox deacon who had fled all the way from the river Don (in southern Russia) on a little cart drawn by a little horse. After the war he sold the horse. Here was someone who should have written a memoir!

As the Germans began to retreat, being caught by the Soviets meant a fate worse, perhaps, than immediate death. The very fact that they had left the "Soviet paradise," made these escapees traitors. They could not be left free in the West. Whenever Soviet troops would capture them, they were automatically repatriated. Some were put to death, if suspected of any connection to the Germans; the rest were placed into concentration camps, mostly in Siberia. All were kept from the rest of the Soviet population so that they wouldn't infect it with their experiences in the West. To a lesser degree, these considerations applied to Poles, Rumanians, Slovaks, Estonians, Latvians, Lithuanians, Bulgarians, Hungarians, and Yugoslavs. Germans too fled the Eastern regions to avoid falling under communism.

These circumstances allowed now unbounded human nature to display itself to its fullest and this final leg from Innsbruck encompassed the entire range of human behaviors. No more veneer of civil social intercourse. Now everyone for himself. But now every manifestation of human kindness, generosity or altruism was pure and unadulterated, as were meanness and selfishness. My mother's memory blotted out manifestations of the latter, but she remembers gratefully some of the former:

I have forgotten much and memories have mingled (my mother wrote these lines when she was eighty-eight). The rest of our odyssey consisted of conveying my son to the Swiss border town of Buchs. We arrived in Feldkirch and slept at the railroad station. Inside the station building all floors were already occupied by exhausted people. We came out on the platform. It was dark now, no benches, a lantern blinked feebly. Where to lie down? Ah, here were some luggage carts — just what we needed. We settled on them under my fur coat. The station fell silent. Snowflakes fluttered. My thoughts mingled in confusion as I fell asleep.

In the morning, we hurried to one of the two little restaurants for some "coffee" and imitation bread (containing a variety of mysterious components, among them some sawdust, but precious little cereal). During the day, I explored the situation and how best to transfer my son into Switzerland. The next night we slept on the customs office's luggage benches. In the morning, a customs officer woke me up. He gave me a thermos with coffee and some crackers: "My wife asked me to give this to you." How to forget this! As I was leaving Europe a few years later, I wrote a warm thank you letter to these kind people.

In those days, Feldkirch and the Lichtenstein/Swiss border, only three kilometers distant, teemed with memorable human scenes. Individuals and groups milled around in an atmosphere of fretful anxiety, all seeking to escape the feared arrival of the Soviets. Some obviously rich and well dressed, some in tattered uniforms of disbanded armies, but mostly drab, haggard, and forlorn civilians.

Conditioned as we are by Hollywood's simplifications — "All Germans Nazis, hence bad, all others good" — the complex emotions of those days now escape us. During the interwar years, many Europeans made intense ideological choices. By 1939, great numbers had cast their lot against communism. Such were, of course, my mother and White Russians, generally. For some others throughout Europe, opposition to communism had led to a fateful alliance with Nazi Germany. They now knew the lethal contingencies: the hour of reckoning had come.

April 29, 1945. Today, I am taking my son to the Lichtenstein/Swiss border. I had always heard that I was "well preserved" and found the four miles across fields to the border an easy walk. The Germans had erected a tall wire-mesh fence across the entire border to impede escapes. There was a gate in it and it led into tiny Lichtenstein, which lay on the way to Buchs, in Switzerland. A crowd of people of various nationalities had gathered in the small open space before that gate awaiting decisions about their destinies. How did these representatives of all countries of Eastern Europe spend the preceding night, on their suitcases? Out of the gate came a young Swiss policeman, clearly not for the first time. He was in charge of this situation and confirmed that if, according to rumors, the Reds were to occupy this area, all would be admitted into Switzerland, but if the French arrived first, the gate into paradise would not open.

The night before, while I slept, I missed some drama at the border. A troop of Russian, ex-Soviet, soldiers arrived. They were immediately admitted into Lichtenstein. Also among those attempting to enter Switzerland was one of the Romanov grand dukes, a pretender to the Russian throne. He and his suite were refused and remained in Feldkirch awaiting destiny.

Other observations at that fateful border. A Lithuanian priest in a cassock being admitted across the border. He stood unsmiling in a sober priestly attitude with his eyes lowered. Only his face shone with happiness. Also two women, one still youngish with a daughter about twenty years old. They too were admitted. There was only joy on their faces. It seemed that they didn't realize their good fortune and were trying to sort out the questions.

I say good-bye to my son. For how long? In hugging him, though I don't easily cry, tears stream down my face. And he, thin and pale, whispers, "Mother, stop crying: everybody sees you and they will laugh."

For me that day remains unforgettable. After crossing the twelve kilometers of Lichtenstein on a train, I alighted in Buchs. It was dark by then. A tall Swiss policeman awaited me. My Swiss godmother had seen to that. He took me to a nearby hotel, where they fed me hot milk, with real white bread and real cheese, none of which I had tasted in weeks, in fact, years. Then they put me to bed in a clean room — the only kind in Switzerland — on a plush mattress covered with a thick, warm duvet cover. I slept.

And now I am alone. I have my fur coat, a handkerchief, a toothbrush and, fortunately, cigarettes. I go to find the Jesuits. They receive me kindly. In Stella Matutina, their monastery/school/farm, I settle the best I can in a room above a hay barn. I eat in the common dining room at a table of the field workers, all of them elderly. All the young men had been conscripted. We eat only vegetables, but in sufficient amounts and I thank God for everything.

My mother was now destitute. She had left most of her belongings in the small Bavarian railroad station, not knowing whether she would see any of it again. Now her only possession was her Turkish Karakul lamb coat, which she considered quite valuable, and of course cigarettes, the only going currency of the day in chaotic Europe. But her life had fitted her well for these trials. She was disciplined and rather ascetic, neither smoked nor drank. At forty-five, she was vigorous, though now undernourished.

The day following my son's departure, I hurried again to the border. I asked the Swiss head of the border office if I could call La Tour de Peilz, my son's new home, at his godmother's. "Oh, you are the lady who cried so much yesterday! Yes, please, of course!" Thereafter I called my son and his "godmother" more than once.

I cannot overlook my meeting Dr. Niehans one day, on the road to the border. He was Swiss, with a Red Cross armband. I introduced myself and he was so kind as to help me obtain very soon a Swiss visa for three weeks. I wanted to see my son, but also visit a bank in Zurich, where I had stowed a modest amount of money before the war, a remnant of my family's flight from Russia in 1920.

In the meantime, the French occupation troops arrived in Feldkirch, to the immense relief of all there who feared communism. I found immediately employment with the French army as an interpreter and secretary. I also established an excellent relationship

111

with my boss, Adjutant Bach, and my life began to normalize in
small Feldkirch, which had remained undamaged by the war. My
son entered a Swiss boarding school and during vacations traveled to
Feldkirch, where he stayed with me. There he also joined the French,
army-sponsored Boy Scouts, read books and hiked in the mountains.

The ending of World War II ushered in an altered universe. In
1918, a chapter had opened that set berserk totalitarian ideologies
on a rampage. In 1945, that chapter closed for two of them: national
socialism and fascism. True, fascism endured in Spain, though
inconsequentially to the international order. Another ideology,
imperialism, a remnant from earlier times, stood on its last legs. That
aging impulse had collapsed in Japan and tottered in the British, Dutch,
and French empires, to vanish in a few short years. The United States
went out of the imperialism business by granting the Philippines its
independence in 1946. In the wake of these transformations only two
ideologies remained: democratic liberal capitalism and totalitarian
communism. Ironically, imperialism's last bastion remained in Stalin's
Soviet Union, which camouflaged it as international communism. The
Bolshevik tsar Stalin had forced Roosevelt's hand and shifted most of
Eastern Europe to the Soviet empire, to submerge these Europeans into
communist despotism.

Now formerly mighty Western Europe, largely ravaged and
impoverished, sought a new self-definition and teetered ideologically
between democracy and communism. Communism expanded
vigorously through its devastated countries, as it also ascended in China.
Democracy flickered, shaken to its ideological foundations, but sought
to regain its footing abetted by the vigor of the United States.

The United States emerged triumphant in 1945, the world's bastion
of democracy and liberal capitalism and increasingly implacable, if
initially bemused, foe of the competing communist ideology. My mother,
as did millions of others across the globe, now developed unreserved
ideological allegiance to the United States.

While continuing to work for the French army, I also pursued
intensely my efforts to extract Father from Belgrade, now in
communist Yugoslavia. A miracle occurred and he returned to me

112

in 1948. I traveled to Innsbruck to find him after his exhausting trip in a third-class car. The poor man had changed profoundly. He was now old, weak, and disoriented, particularly after several days on a train through still desolated Yugoslavia — a man whom I remember as a formidable intellectual force and an imposing physical presence. During one change of trains he had lost his glasses. I brought him to Feldkirch, where I found him a warm and comfortable room.

Of course, no miracle occurred. My mother merely applied dogged persistence and skillful and imaginative initiatives in the face of seemingly insuperable obstacles. As on that day in Munich when she entered the only door whose Eintritt was verboten, she left no stone unturned, even stones otherwise invisible.

Soon, we received an Argentine visa and all three embarked on a ship in Marseille. Argentina welcomed freely all who had suffered from the war, while we would have had to wait eight years for an American visa. Thus we left Europe.

Reaching Harbor

My mother's memoir, though not her life, largely ends here. She was now forty-eight and she lived for another forty-one years, the first fourteen of them in Argentina. Her destiny removed her henceforth from her European cultural home and from European events.

As I mention in *At the Whirlpool's Edge*, Mr. Pogoretzki, who courted my mother in Belgrade, prudently decided to leave Europe in 1939 and spent World War II peacefully in Argentina. After the war, he managed to find my mother while she worked for the French troops in Austria and invited her to come to Argentina. By then, things looked grim again in Europe. The Soviets had blockaded access to Berlin and Truman began the epic airlift into the besieged city. Internal communisms threatened Western countries from within, bringing fear of a possible Soviet invasion. A war atmosphere had descended on the continent and my mother judged it prudent to leave Europe. Accepting Mr. Pogoretzki's invitation seemed wise.

> *For the ocean voyage I obtained a second-class berth for Father. My son spent all nineteen days of the crossing sleeping on a bench on the deck and I slept in steerage. We were leaving Europe without knowing Spanish and with a small reserve of money, not the best practical preparation for a new life. But to experience another war in Europe seemed beyond what human strength could endure.*

Fleeing in cattle wagons, boarding panicky trains through windows and, to complete the refugee experience, my mother now traveled to the New World in classic immigrant fashion — in steerage. Her life never lacked in drama and neither did our landing in Buenos Aires. While we were crossing the ocean, Mr. Pogoretzki died of a heart attack. On arrival, we knew no one in the new land. Now my mother faced life with a senile father and an uncertain teenager. Once again, a struggle to establish an existence.

Father passed quietly away eight months later. He was eighty-six, in a fog of senility, much weakened by his adventures of recent years. In June 1950, North Korea invaded South Korea and started the Korean War. I was now very glad to have decided to immigrate to Argentina. My son was now nineteen and had we immigrated to the United States, he would have been drafted and sent to war. Had we stayed in France, he would have been drafted and sent to fight in Indo-China.

As at earlier stages in her odysseys, my mother needed work to survive and she began to cast about. She learned how to make stuffed toy animals and contracted with a toy store in Buenos Aires to supply them with bears, rabbits, and like fauna. But fairly soon she returned to teaching French, a popular interest among educated Argentines, and opened a branch of the Alliance Française, the French government's worldwide chain of French schools. She formed a new life, but never sank roots in a country completely alien to her Russian and Western European cultural outlook. I worked and studied. Being young and knowing a couple of other Latin languages, I learned Spanish quickly. For my mother this was more difficult and her Spanish was never flawless.

She built a small house in a Buenos Aires suburb. Instead of flowers and fruit trees, the house's garden functioned as a mini zoo, as did, in fact, the house. Once on the land, my mother gave full rein to her instincts for saving stray animals. These abounded in Argentina: mangy dogs, wounded cats, even a bat and a damaged horse. My mother's wounded soul couldn't behold the sight of suffering. She poured her compassion into other defenseless creatures.

Her memoir, now contracting, contains a residual about the Russian civil war:

In 1956, I met Baron (last name illegible). He and his wife lived in Córdoba, in provincial Argentina. In 1919, the Bolsheviks arrested and imprisoned him when he was a young Russian officer. He shared a cell with four (Romanov) grand dukes, whom the Bolsheviks went out of their way to torture and humiliate. Baron ... told me that when the grand dukes were taken to their execution, they marched off in silent dignity. He was saved by his wife, who immediately upon his arrest hurried to see (the great leftist novelist) Maxim Gorky, whom Lenin held in high esteem. Gorky interceded with Lenin and Baron ... was freed. He told me that to this day he is ashamed that he never went to thank Gorky for having saved his life. He was afraid that fellow Whites would misinterpret this contact with the enemy.

There was also romance. My mother met a good man, a Russian who had survived five years of a German concentration camp. They had a hesitant relationship through much of 1950s, but she would not commit to marriage. Both ulcerated souls bled sorrow and regrets. It didn't seem possible, at least to her, that a normal matrimony could ensue.

In 1960, my son, having obtained an education, left for the United States. Two years later, I joined him in California to undertake yet another new life.

For a last time, my mother began to make a wrenching adjustment. Her years in America became lonely, since she found it difficult to make new friends at her age. We didn't have much money (in American parlance, we were "poor") and my mother returned to teaching languages. She started a little language school in Menlo Park, in California, taught French and Russian herself, and hired other teachers for other languages. It never prospered, because she completely lacked any commercial instinct, so indispensable in America.

She became an American citizen and developed a genuine affection for America and its people, whom she perceived as virtuous, certainly by comparison with all her preceding experiences. She also grew a deep commitment to democracy, which she understood as egalitarian and compassionate — an interesting evolution from her socially privileged early years in autocratic Russia. She cheered the American man on the moon in 1969 and generally took great interest in public affairs in her new country.

In 1971, I visited Europe again, with my son. We went to Wenduyne-sur-Mer, in Belgium. That was the wonderful resort where World War I caught my family and me on August 1, 1914. Now, fifty-six years later, Belgium is poorer. The charming villas have disappeared or have been converted into pensions. Among them still stands a World War II German gun emplacement.

After that, we paid one last visit to our farm in the Provence, which I had sold in the meantime. The sight of it brought back contradictory feelings. My son was born and my husband died there. I had spent nine, at times happy, years in that house. At the birth of my son, I had planted a row of young cypresses. Forty years later, they had grown into giants.

In late 1916, (Mrs.) Elena Bezak had organized a play, Children to Children, to raise funds for war orphans, in which I had participated (see above, The Great War – Life's First Lessons). Unfathomable destiny reunited us over half a century later in San Francisco. Not long thereafter Mrs. Bezak, who was quite old by then, passed away and was buried in the Serbian-Russian cemetery in San Francisco. I have recently purchased a plot in that cemetery not far from hers. How could we have imagined in Kiev, in 1916, such a preposterous ending to our lives?

My mother longed for Russia, but she would not consider visiting the communist Soviet Union. In 1969, she did the next best thing and took a cruise to Alaska to visit what once was Russian land. Specifically she went to Sitka, then the capital of Russian Alaska and visited the churches and the cemeteries. These ghostly links to her land moved her greatly and she wrote a substantial article for a San Francisco Russian newspaper.

I wished greatly in 1988 to travel to Kiev to witness the celebration of one thousand years of Russian Christianity, but my son convinced me not to go. "The sight of your house may kill you of sorrow." My friend Maria Gagarina went, but she has a different character! So we didn't go...

April 14, 1989. My son just called from Philadelphia, where he travels on business. He told me that he took a taxi, the driver of which turned out to be not only Russian, but also from Kiev. My son asked him whether he knew the address of his mother's house and he did, though the street name had changed. He also asked the taxi driver whether he knew Father's clinic. Oh, yes, he said, Professor Lapinski's clinic. So the medical establishment is ignoring Father, but the people remember. How pleasing to hear this!

I am saddened not to have taken my mother to Kiev. Had I but known that in 1988 the communists were on their knees! When in 2004 I visited Kiev, her house still stood, well kept, now in a new country, Ukraine, a country she would not have acknowledged, Russian patriot that she was.

My mother died in late September 1989. Four weeks later the Berlin Wall collapsed and only democratic liberal capitalism remained standing. With this concluded the actual, if not the calendric twentieth century. I am also saddened that my mother didn't witness that moment when the last totalitarian ideology of the twentieth century entered its death throes. How this would have pleased her!

Made in the USA
Charleston, SC
07 June 2011